"Sheryl is a woman who has lived depending on God by having a deep abiding understanding of His names. If you want a solid foundation to build a life on, dive into the pages of this book."

~Pam Farrel, author of 7 *Simple Skills for Every Woman: Success in Keeping It All Together*

"If you long to draw close to God, I challenge you to engage in this 31-day experience of studying the power and presence of God through understanding His names. Sheryl Giesbrecht skillfully reveals how we can engage with our personal, intimate, all-knowing and all-powerful God. This study will transform your life."

~Carol Kent, speaker and author
***When I Lay My Isaac Down* (NavPress)**

"*Experiencing God Through His Names* is a very important book. Most of us aren't very aware of the names of God because the meaning of names isn't valued. But Sheryl Giesbrecht's book will change that. I love how she includes little personal vignettes and then takes us into biblical explanations of each of God's names. This devotional is a book we all can read and refer to time and time again."

~Kathy Collard Miller, speaker and author of *Choices of the Heart: Daughters of the King Bible study series*

"What better way to know God more intimately than through learning and studying His names? Sheryl Giesbrecht has written a beautiful devotional every believer needs. She helps us experience God on a deeper, more compelling level, ultimately enabling us to know Him more."

~Julie K. Gillies, author of *Prayers for a Woman's Soul*

"Let's face it; we need help navigating this complicated and stressful life. Sheryl Giesbrecht invites you to find that wisdom and power in her latest book *Experiencing God Through His Names*. Sheryl captivates the reader's heart as she unpacks how fulfilling and exciting it is when we take time to bask in God's presence and reflect on His trustworthy and loving character. Sheryl found this strength and courage when she was a young mom and needed help during difficult and painful parts of her journey. In a style that is personal and laced with deep insight and grace, her stories ring true because she has walked every aspect of this book. What a great tool for a group study or meaningful personal times of solitude and reflection. Highlight your favorite sections and allow them to carry you through each day with renewed understanding of the love and greatness of our God."

~Heidi McLaughlin, speaker and author of *Sand to Pearls, Restless for More*

"Knowing facts about God in your head, is completely different from knowing Him personally and intimately. "Experiencing God Through His Names" will enable you to develop a closeness with God as you get to know Him through His many names used in Scripture. Sheryl has such an uncanny ability to combine Bible passages, her personal stories and then apply everything in a way that will expand your faith and strengthen your walk with God. If you want to enrich your relationship with God, this is a must read. Sheryl has a heart for God which makes all those who meet her and read her books, to want that same tender heart."

~Pastor Sharon Hurkens, author of *Exit the Wilderness, Just for Today, Jesus is Enough*

"Sheryl Giesbrecht opened her heart and shared poignant scenes from her life to illustrate names of God in the Bible. As you read, you'll be encouraged and enabled to face the darkest storms. Highly recommended."

~Cynthia L Simmons, Heart of the Matter Radio host, author of *Pursuing Gold*

"It's easy to become overwhelmed by the daily pressures and responsibilities we encounter. As a mother and busy ministry leader, Sheryl knows those pressures well. In *Experiencing God Through His Names*, she invites us to walk with her from a state of busyness into personal breakthrough. She not only leads you into a time of devotion and praising God, but also gives life-changing practical applications of how God through his names affects our parenting, marriages, and careers."

~Saundra Dalton-Smith MD, speaker and author of
Come Empty: Pour Out Life's Hurts and
Receive God's Healing Love

"This book is a powerful, fresh breath of hope, drawing us deep into the very heart of God. Sheryl's love of the Lord and intimate knowledge of His Word creates a 31-day feast, strengthening our faith with reminders of God's lavish love and overcoming power."

~Kelly Hall, Director of women's ministry, speaker,
author of *Courageous Faith*

Experiencing God

Through His Names

Experiencing God Through

His Names

Sheryl D. Giesbrecht

Published in the USA

ISBN 978-0692743010

Bold Vision Books
PO Box 2011
Friendswood, Texas 77549

Cover by litfuse
Interior design by kae Creative Solutions

Dedication

Affectionately dedicated to my mother,
Shirley Adkins. Mom showed me how to
wait on God and listen for His voice. She
taught me to pray using His Word and
helped me learn to call on Him by name.

"Glorify the Lord with me;
let us exalt his name together."
Psalm 34:3

Table of Contents

Foreword

Books have the potential of coming alongside us and becoming good friends. We may even get a sense that "this book was written especially for me." Even then, books have limitations as long as the conversation is one-sided. This excellent book by Sheryl Giesbrecht takes us far beyond that.

Information about the names of God are often presented to us in a list. Seeing the names, and what they mean, listed is delightfully overwhelming, but you also feel as if you're waving at God as you drive by. We need opportunities to stop the car, go in the house, and talk with the God who embodies these things.

So this book invites us not only to read the information but also to do something with it so that we have the opportunity to experience God. This happens as we interact with God about the truths behind these names. We can pause and tell God what we're thinking and ask God for more input. Reading this book and interacting with God then becomes a three-way conversation among the author, God and the reader. Or we might even find that the reading causes us to respond to God in worship. This is ideal because study (even reading a book) and worship go together. Study without worship produces arrogance and worship without study often results in fluff.

So I'm glad that Sheryl Giesbrecht offers us not only exceptional information with very down-to-earth ideas about the names of God but also leads us to pray in light of how this new information invites us into new ways of embracing God. When prayers are based on such solid truth, they become deeper in substance and combine prayer and worship as well as straight-up delight.

Out of such interaction with Jesus flows an organic response in which the truth permeates our life so that we think and act differently. Experiencing God through those divine designations and affectionate appellations brings us into partnership with God in loving the world God so loves. Jesus no doubt did this as he embraced all of who God was in prayer. So as we read Experiencing God through his Names, and pray in that way, we pray in the name of Jesus, in the presence of Jesus, in the power of Jesus, even in the reality of Jesus.

~Jan Johnson

**Retreat Speaker and Author of *Meeting God in Scripture, When the Soul Listens,* and *Invitation to the Jesus Life*
www.JanJohnson.org**

Acknowledgments

I wish to express my deepest appreciation to my husband, Jim Turner for his constant love, support, and encouragement for me to diligently study and accurately teach God's word.

To Sue Sabaloni for inviting me to join the Longfellow Moms In Touch group and teaching me how to pray using the names of God.

To the memory and legacy of the late Peggy Turner for encouraging me to buy the Moms In Touch leaders' guide for my personal growth to help me pray using the names of God.

To honor and remember the heritage of my first husband, the late Paul Giesbrecht, who during the year of my stage-four cancer treatment boosted my confidence to continue studying and writing in spite of how I felt.

To Vickie Sanford for her example in praying the names of God faithfully in her private prayer time and with me in our prayer times.

To Sheryle Saunders, Sandy Darrow, Ruth Anderson, Lori Taylor, Annie Vlach, Raylene Duke, and the thousands of moms worldwide, who join in praying for our children through Moms In Touch (now Moms In Prayer).

To Carol Wilcox for her attention to details and for faithfully praying for God's word to go forth.

To my far-flung family and friends from Bakersfield, California to Bujumbura, Burundi and beyond, thank you for your love, friendship, and commitment to hold me up in prayer.

To my ministry partners through the radio airwaves and cyber connections, thank you for your passion for the lost so all men and women will personally know and call on the name of God.

"Ascribe to the Lord the glory due his name;
worship the Lord in the splendor of his holiness."

Psalm 29:2

A Word from Sheryl

I was a stressed out pastor's wife, working a job outside of our home, mothering a preschooler and kindergartener, and exhausted from the demands of my family and ministry. I needed support and friends. I joined a Moms In Touch group (now known as Moms in Prayer International www.momsinprayer.org). This phenomenal group of women loved to pray and taught me how to worship God by praying His names. This practice not only deepened my prayer life, it increased my faith. I've become more acquainted with God's character and every day I actively seek to trust Almighty God.

Spiritually, something exciting and personal happens when we study God's names, we find out about His unique character qualities and experience His Holy Spirit presence. In the next few weeks, we will take time to examine these special names of God, one by one. So glad you can join me for a 31-day experience as we draw close to God. I can't wait for you to find out how God will show you more of His power and presence. If you haven't ever studied the names of God, you are in for a treat. Imagine looking at a postcard of the Grand Canyon. The solo shots each show a segment of a breathtaking view. When we absorb truths about God one at a time, we can better understand the reality and certainty of His character and the capability of His presence in our daily lives.

During the next few weeks, we will journey together to:

* Understand 31 of God's names

* Experience God's power in fresh ways

* Explain 31 of God's names to others

* Increase our desire for intimacy with God

17

*Apply our experience with God to other areas of life – parenting, marriage, marketplace and personal communication

Each of the names of God reveal something about His character. Understanding God's titles reveals His purposes and His commitment to us and gives us practical handles for life applications. Exodus 20:24 says, "Wherever I cause My name to be honored, I will come to you and bless you." God wants us to understand Him as we study His character through His names.

Take a minute to underline Exodus 20:24 in your Bible, and let's pray:

> Heavenly Father, I honor your name, I bless your name, I praise your name. I pray for your wisdom, discipline, and insight as I embark on the journey of knowing you by Your names. Lord, I want to experience you more. Thank you for your willingness in allowing me to find you. In Jesus' Name, amen.

Day 1 Father

B e careful, sweetie," my dad's strong voice cautioned me to avoid the object in the road. He'd just removed the training wheels on my Schwinn; so even though I was seated securely on the banana seat, both hands on the handlebars, the front tire still wobbled a little. I focused intently on the path ahead, "Yes, Father," I said. I veered to the left just a little and swerved to avoid the obstacle.

Father is one of the most familiar names for God. Father is God's distinguishing title in the New Testament. In Matthew 6, Jesus taught the disciples how to pray in the verses we know as the Lord's Prayer. He began, "Our Father in heaven," giving honor and worth to his Father God. "Our Father in Heaven" gives us the image of God in His majestic and holy place, reminding us He is personal, loving, and involved with our lives.

Father is the most commonly used name of God.

And I will be a Father to you, and you will be my sons and daughters, says the Lord Almighty (2 Corinthians 6:18).

For you did not receive the spirit of bondage again to fear, but you received the Spirit of adoption by whom we cry out, "Abba, Father." The Spirit himself bears witness with our spirit that we are children of God" (Romans 8:15-16 NKJV).

It's amazing that the Almighty God of Heaven wants us to call Him Father.

Perhaps your hurts and hang-ups toward your own earthly father have clouded your view of the Heavenly Father. If you have experienced a dysfunctional family, emotional or physical abuse, you, too probably view your God through this grid. As you understand biblical truth about God and His character, you will begin to believe that God's character is reliable, unchanging, and faithful.

The Old Testament Jews did not think of God as an intimate father. In fact, they had no concept of the fatherhood of God. When Jesus talked about His intimate oneness with God the Father, it was startling and revolutionary. The Old Testament (OT) Jews observed the Lord God Almighty, the One who dwelt between the cherubim. (See Psalm 80:1.) He was a whirlwind of fire, a fearful God, punishing the sinner. The Lord God of the OT was to be feared because he represented judgment. He killed Uzziah when he touched the Ark, punished Moses for disobedience; did not allow Moses to enter the Promised Land, and allowed Nebuchadnezzar to destroy Jerusalem because the Jews worshiped idols and committed fornication. Hebrews 12:29 says "Our God is a consuming fire." Scary, huh? Far from Father-like. Maybe you can relate.

The Father-heart of God is revealed in the Luke 15 story of a father who had two sons. The prodigal son took one-third of the family inheritance, insulting his upbringing, his father, and his family name by his request, yet the father gave him what he asked. The young prodigal squandered his wealth on partying. When he had nothing left, he worked for his keep in a pig sty. He faced a dramatic reality check, "When he finally came to his senses, he said to himself, 'At home, even the hired servants have food enough to spare and here I am, dying of hunger!'" (Luke 15:17 NLT).

Left with no other alternatives, the prodigal son returned home—filthy, broke, and ashamed—to confess to his father what he had done. In the same way, each of us was a disobedient runaway, independently making unhealthy choices. Our Father waited for us, saw us in the distance, ran toward us, fell upon our necks, and kissed us. Through God's grace, we were restored immediately. He continues to welcome us home and restores us into relationship with Him.

When we come to the Father, our credentials are unacceptable, our faithfulness is fickle, and our return may be under questionable motive. Yet our Father takes us in and asks no questions. Instead, He celebrates us. He tells us not to worry. He has given us hope for a future beyond all expectations. He wants us to celebrate His goodness and His presence in our lives as our Father.

Let's pray.

> Thank you, Father, for allowing me to call you such an endearing name. I praise, worship and call on you, Father. In Jesus name, amen.

Day 2 Elohim

I couldn't stop staring. I was captivated by the perfection of my infant daughter's features and fingers, even her dainty little toes. I lifted my praise to Creator God, "I worship you, God for allowing me to be a mother to this precious life."

I remember another time I couldn't stop staring. It happened years before, as a Bible school student. I'd been given an assignment in our theology class to worship God, outdoors, after dark, to contemplate the power of God as it is revealed in the magnitude of the heavens. The professor's instruction for our stargazing assignment was to lay flat on our backs, look up into the sky and meditate on Psalm 139 while meditating on God's greatness. Have you ever marveled over the vastness of the heavens? This kind of practice helps us remain in awe and amazement of the power of our Creator.

Elohim is the name of God that means "all-powerful Creator." The same great Elohim made us to specifically and individually fulfill His purposes.

Used over 2,500 times in the Old Testament, Elohim reveals God to us in numerous ways. Elohim created everything out of nothing, the Latin term is *Ex Nihilo*, evidencing His creative power and might in creating the whole universe in six days. Each day Elohim gives us evidence to remind us of His presence and endless inventiveness.

The miracle of new life reminds us of the supremacy of our Elohim. As we contemplate the preciousness of birth, we are brought to a more acute awareness of our Creator. It's not surprising that the Psalmist writes, "I praise you because I am [we are] fearfully and wonderfully made; your works are wonderful, I know that full well" (Psalm 139:14).

It is most appropriate that by this name (Elohim) God should reveal Himself-bringing cosmos out of chaos, light out of darkness, habitation out of desolation, and life in His image.[1]

Consider the ways Elohim (Creator God) is asking you to trust Him in the circumstances of your life. He has planned each of your days and ordered all of your ways.

> All the days ordained for me were written in your book before one of them came to be (Psalm 139:16).

Commit to allowing the Creator to use your situations to make you more like Jesus. Submit yourself to Elohim who created you. God's eyes are on us all the time, a reason to invest time in the practice of worship, gazing and directing our praise to the Creator.

Let's pray.

> Dear Elohim, I praise you for being my Creator. I worship Your power and might. Thank You for making me just the way You planned. Thank You for the good gifts You have given me. Thank You for the ways You have been faithful to me. I commit the circumstances of this day to Your powerful presence. May Your will be done in all I do and say today. Help me direct my gaze and my praise to you alone. In Jesus name, amen.

Day 3 El Elyon

It was the last week of the month. Now self-employed, my husband Paul had been without work for about four months. Bill collectors had been calling all week. After paying our rent, somehow I'd managed to pay the minimum amount on our water service and credit cards. We'd been unable to pay our gas and electric bill for two months, now it was so high, I couldn't wrap my mind around how we would pay it. I wondered when our power would be shut off. And there were less than thirty dollars left in our checking account. How would we feed our family? Sometimes our problems seem bigger than God. When God is worshiped, praised, and elevated to His rightful place in our lives, these 'giants' are put into perspective. "I cry out to God Most High, to God, who fulfills His purpose for me" (Psalm 57:2 ESV).

The name of God—El Elyon, the Most High God—reminds us who God is and what He has done. As long as we traverse the earth, we will fight battles and face problems. Like enemy ogres attacking, they invade our thoughts, interrupt harmony in our relationships, and intrude on our peace. No matter what we're up against, God is bigger than any giant we might fear. El Elyon is the name of God that means the Most High God. It is used about 40 times in the Old Testament

Most high means supreme God or most loved God. In Genesis 14, Abraham was up against insurmountable odds—318 household servants fighting the most powerful armies of Kedorlaomer. God can't be overshadowed even when our giants seem bigger than God. With God on our side, we have the success. El Elyon was responsible for Abram's victory over his enemies. God delivered the enemy armies into Abram's hand.

When you face battles, let El Elyon bring to mind the verses such as, "You will keep in perfect peace, those whose minds are steadfast, because they trust in you" (Isaiah 26:3). Ask God for the strength to keep your mind on Him. When your mind wanders, intentionally refocus it back to God and His presence. Concentrating on Him may be difficult when we are tired, and we feel we don't have the physical or mental resources we need, but El Elyon, the Most High God, is big enough to shield us from everything that wants to run us down, including ourselves. "Abram gave God the credit for his success. He wanted his ungodly neighbors to see how God blessed him; he wanted them to realize that he served "the Lord, the most high God."[2]

El Elyon, the God Most High, is the only One who can deliver us from our enemies. He will invade our enemies, take captive our thoughts and win our battles. Let's give God credit for our victory. Others will notice, as did the King of Salem, Melchizedek. "And he blessed Abram, saying, 'Blessed be Abram by God Most High, creator of heaven and earth. And blessed be God Most High, who delivered your enemies into your hand'" (Genesis 14:19).

I won't forget that night when my family had too much month left at the end of our money. We prayed together for God to provide for us. And He did exactly that very thing. Unexpected checks arrived in our mailbox, and family members offered to babysit for free, so I could save money on childcare. Because we were given so many gently-worn hand-me-down clothes, I didn't have to shop for school clothes for the kids. The God Most High came through again.

Let's let El Elyon have his rightful place in our lives as the God Most High. As we elevate Him, the shadow of the Most High will cover our giants with His presence, minimizing them to a manageable capacity. You don't have to live under your circumstances. With El Elyon, the God Most High, you can rise above your circumstances.

Let's pray.

> Dear El Elyon, I recognize you as the God Most High. You are the only One who can deliver me from my enemies. Your ways are not my ways. Thank you for the truth in Psalm 46:10a, "Be still and know that I am God." Help me to be still and let you fight my battles. In Jesus name, amen.

Day 4 El Olam

"To infinity and beyond," proclaimed *Toy Story* hero Buzz Lightyear as he blasted off from his battery-powered plastic pedestal, only to end his maiden voyage by crashing into the ceiling. Buzz' boastful wish was to travel faster than the speed of light to conquer worlds unlimited by time or space. Yet, his efforts were stopped by an impenetrable force.

In real life, the concept of "infinity and beyond" challenges human understanding, yet is a welcome exercise to our spiritual imagination. The infinity symbol according to Wikipedia is sometimes called the *lemniscate*. It is a mathematical symbol representing the concept of infinity. It has no beginning or end. This same symbol is also used to illustrate the eternal concept of God, as an eternal being, since He has no beginning or end. The *lemniscate* symbol is inadequate because it begins and ends upon itself. Like Buzz Lightyear's failed attempt to soar into the outer limits, our attempt to wrap our minds around God's eternal nature might be blocked by hitting the ceiling of our intellectual understanding. A better illustration might be a line that has no beginning or end. God's eternal nature is limitless, humanly unfathomable, and has no glass ceiling. "All history is but a speck within the spectrum of eternity. El Olam transcends all time." [3] "..he remains faithful forever" (Psalm 146:6).

It's generous of God to give us glimpses of Himself to help us understand His eternal character. He loves us with an everlasting love (Psalm 103:17), offers us eternal life (John 3:16), provides never-ending comfort and hope (2 Thessalonians 2:16), and supplies endless promises that He always keeps (Psalm 146:6). The thousands of decisions you and I make each day do make a difference for eternity.

Has anyone ever failed to follow through for you? Life is full of people who break promises, cause disappointment and bring on frustration. God will never break a promise. El Olam keeps every promise He has ever made to us. Our part is to know exactly what those promises are.

El Olam was in the beginning and will exist until time comes to an end. Abraham respected the truth of God's eternity by planting a tree as an act of worship.

> Abraham planted a tamarisk tree at Beersheba, and he worshiped the Lord, the Eternal God (Genesis 21:33).

What a comfort to have a relationship with the Eternal One, El Olam.

The saying, "Only one life will soon be past, but only what is done for Christ will last" helps us understand that if we focus on His eternal plans while we live our lives on earth, our toil is not in vain. Someday, we will be with Him. Time, as we know it, will cease. We will understand the meaning of "infinity and beyond," and what we now understand by faith will be reality. We will dwell with Him, not just for a year, ten, or twenty, but forever. We will live with El Olam, the Eternal One, for eternity, infinity, and beyond.

Let's pray.

> Dear El-Olam, thank You for this aspect of Your personality as our Eternal God. This fact

of Your existence gives perspective not just to my life but also to my problems. I praise You for keeping Your promises, honoring Your commitments and sustaining me through the changes and challenges of life. Help me keep this eternal sense of awareness today. In Jesus name, amen.

Day 5 El Roi

Run away, escape, flee were the only solutions desperate Hagar could devise. Sarai chose Hagar to bear Abraham's child. Hagar was merely following orders. Now pregnant, her jealous mistress abused her. Hagar's challenges had been brought on by other people's choices. Despised, mistreated, and abandoned, Hagar decided to run away.

They will never find me, Hagar thought as she escaped into the desert. Blindly heading for unknown territory and anonymity, she left the security of food and shelter. Instead of facing her circumstances, she chose to run, yet was unable to get away from herself. Lost in the desert, Hagar was wrenched with hunger, agonizing over the baby. The wilderness was terrifying. Physically exhausted and emotionally spent, she collapsed by a spring in the desert. It was there the angel of the Lord found Hagar. She couldn't escape God. "Hagar, servant of Sarai, where have you come from, and where are you going?" boomed the voice of the angel of the Lord in Genesis 16:8.

"I am running away from my mistress Sarai," Hagar cried, covering her eyes from the angel's radiance. The angel told Hagar to go back, face Sarai and submit to her. Listening intently, with awe and wonder, Hagar received a blessing and a promise about the future of her unborn child. "I will increase your descendants so much that they will be too numerous to count…. You are now pregnant, and you will give birth to a son. You shall name him Ishmael, for the Lord has heard of your misery" (Genesis 16:10,11).

Hagar experienced God. "She gave this name to the Lord who spoke to her: 'You are the God who sees me,' for she said, 'I have now seen the One who sees me.'" (Genesis 16:13). She called the Lord "El Roi—the One who sees me" and Hagar named the place of the God-sighting Beer Lahai Roi. God had seen Hagar's pain and heard her cries. "El Roi" is the name of God, which means "The God Who Sees." El Roi saw barren Sarai convince Abram to have a child with Hagar, her Egyptian servant. El Roi saw the abuses Hagar experienced at the hands of jealous Sarai. El Roi saw Hagar flee into the desert doomed to die. El Roi revealed Himself, prophesying the nation to come from the birth of her son, Ishmael. "I have seen the One who sees me" (Genesis 16:13).

El Roi is still "The God Who Sees." He sees us in our depression, desperation, and difficulty. Maybe you don't consider yourself as someone with a break-and-run mentality like Hagar, but you have denied there is a problem or avoided the problem by finding other things to talk about. To face a problem means to admit it, and then to consider ways to solve it.

El Roi sees everything and knows everything; He knows and understands all that happens. "For the eyes of the Lord range throughout the earth to strengthen those whose hearts are fully committed to him" (2 Chronicles 16:9). Hagar experienced this strengthening when she believed God's promise and received His blessing over her child. Although Hagar ran from a very difficult and messy situation, El Roi found her in the wilderness and helped her in returning to an impossible situation.

El Roi sees us in impossible circumstances. When we face our obstacles with His help, we know He will work all things out for good. Instead of running from problems, run into the arms of El Roi—The God Who Sees. He will hold you close and give you strength to face every difficulty for His glory!

> And we know that in all things God works for the good of those who love him, who have been called according to his purpose (Romans 8:28).

Let's pray.

> Heavenly Father, thank you El Roi—the God Who Sees. I cannot run away from You. I am utterly amazed when I try to get away, you seek after me to gather me back to You but furthermore, You are waiting for me in the destination I've chosen for my escape. Thank You that because of your compassion, Your eyes of love never let me out of Your sight. and Your gaze follows me wherever I flee. You sustain my every need until I come running back to You—arms, heart, and eyes wide open to be reunited with You. I tried to hide from You, but you never let me out of Your sightnd You won't ever let me go. In Jesus name, amen.

Day 6 El Shaddai

Late last night, my husband, Jim and I were outside underneath a pitch black velvet sky, dotted with thousands of twinkling stars. Like an infinite shimmering canopy over our heads, we were caught up in amazement and stunned by the majestic heavenly expression of God's power. We were reminded of El Shaddai, the name of God that means "The Almighty, All-Sufficient God."

El Shaddai is the name of God that means God is sufficient for the needs of His people. El Shaddai, Abram's God, is our Almighty God, who is sufficient to provide for every need, even what seems impossible.

I found a great definition of El Shaddai in The Blue Letter Bible:

> God Shaddai; *pantokratôr* (for Shaddai) —the Almighty. *El* is another name that is translated as "God" and can be used in conjunction with other words to designate various aspects of God's character. Another word much like *Shaddai*, and from which many believe it derived, is shad meaning "breast" in Hebrew (some other scholars believe that the name is derived from an Akkadian word *Šadu*, meaning "mountain," suggesting strength and power). This refers to God completely nourishing, satisfying, and supplying His people with all their needs as a mother would her child. Connected with

the word for God, *El*, this denotes a God who freely gives nourishment and blessing, He is our sustainer.

"When Abram was ninety-nine years old, the Lord appeared to him and said, "I am God Almighty [El Shaddai], walk before me faithfully and be blameless. Then I will make my covenant between me and you and will greatly increase your numbers" (Genesis 17:1-2).

El Shaddai is not only Almighty God, powerful and sustaining, His mighty presence intersects with His other character qualities, specifically El Olam—The Eternal God.

In His immense command and nourishing strength, El Olam keeps His promises, and El Shaddai follows through with what He says he will do.

> Abram fell facedown, and God said to him, "As for me, this is my covenant with you: you will be the father of many nations. No longer will you be called Abram, your name will be called Abraham, for I have made you a father of many nations. I will make you very fruitful, I will make nations of you, and kings will come from you" (Genesis 17:3-6).

Imagine the commanding voice of God speaking to Abraham. Unable to stand in His presence, Abraham fell flat on his face. God revealed Himself and explained what would happen next. God's revelation to Abraham resulted in a deeper relationship because Abraham became God's friend. El Shaddai was especially familiar to the patriarchs—Abraham, Isaac, and Jacob.

God reveals Himself to us through His names, so that we can know Him better. When we think of El Shaddai, it sounds like the word "shudder or shuddering," and could lead to the spiritual response of soul "shaking, trembling, quaking," because of our awe and wonder of God's tremendous power. We, too, might also feel compelled to respond with a physical reaction of worship, humility, or respect—not out of fear, but of reverence for His majesty.

Our finite minds are stretched when we attempt to comprehend the power of El Shaddai. It helps to experience Him in nature.

As we face challenges ahead, it's refreshing to let God, El Shaddai—The Almighty, All Sufficient One, take our heavy load. El Shaddai is the God who is enough. Let's worship Him in the creation and allow His presence to encircle us with His mighty power. Surrounded by this strength, His presence ushers in peace which enfolds the decisions and difficulties of the day. We are energized by El Shaddai's enormous clout, giving us renewed hope as we walk into the purposes according to His plans.

By His power, God can accomplish anything, above all we could ever think.

> Now all glory to God, who is able, through his mighty power at work within us, to accomplish infinitely more than we might ask or think (Ephesians 3:20 NLT).

El Shaddai, Abram's God, is our Almighty God, who is sufficient to provide the impossible. El Shaddai is more than able; He is the God who is more than enough.

Let's pray.

El Shaddai, thank You for Your mighty power at work in me. You are more than able to accomplish more than I could ever dare ask or hope. Thank You for Your sufficiency, ability, nourishment, friendship. Thank You for who You are, El Shaddai. May Your presence and peace keep me close to You today. I pray I will make a difference today because You are my El Shaddai. In Jesus name, amen.

Day 7 Adonai

Have you ever second-guessed a decision you've made? Me too. In my time alone with God today, He reminded me, "Sheryl, release the decisions swirling in your anxious mind. I am your master." Today we are marinating on the promises found in the name of God, Adonai.

Our God, Adonai is the supreme master over all authorities, and we belong to Him. We can trust this sovereign Lord, master Adonai to direct our lives and guide our actions. This authoritative title is translated Master, Lord, or Sovereign. To abide in the living God, Adonai, we must say yes to His lordship over our lives. We can trust His kind direction and abide in peace as He guides our decisions.

The Blue Letter Bible explains:

> In the Old Testament Adonai occurs 434 times. There are many uses of Adonai in Isaiah (e.g., Adonai Jehovah). It occurs 200 times in Ezekiel alone and appears 11 times in Daniel. Adonai is the verbal parallel to Yahweh and Jehovah. Adonai is plural; the singular is adon. In reference to God, the plural Adonai is used. When the singular adon is used, it usually refers to a human lord. "Thou shalt not take the name of the LORD thy God in vain" (Exodus 20:7), sometimes Adonai was used as a substitute for Yahweh (YHWH). Adonai can be translated literally as, "my lords' " (both plural and possessive).

If you've ever rented a house, you remember what it was like to live with the landlord's (the master's) rules. You took good care of your rental, you asked permission before you painted the walls, and the landlord made the repairs. That's the way it is when we submit our "temple," our body, to Adonai. We are not our own. God is a gracious landlord, who has given us boundaries for living. When we follow the Master's rules and stay within his boundaries, we walk in his will and abide in his peace.

Exalt and praise Adonai, our Sovereign Master, worthy of the highest honor and our total obedience. Because of Jesus' obedience on the cross, you and I have been "bought with a price." (See 1 Corinthians 16:20.) The apostle Paul called himself a "bond-servant of Jesus Christ," meaning someone who willingly chose to serve his master, belonging to his owner with no freedom to leave. Jesus came to live His life on earth as a servant of God. His example speaks to us. He told his disciples, "My food…is to do the will of Him who sent me and to finish His work" (John 4:34).

Trust Adonai by completely submitting and surrendering your time, talent, and treasure to Him. Let Him be Lord and Master of your life, because reliance on His authority ushers us into a place of confidence and hope. Peace is a result when we submit to God fully and serve Him as good stewards of all He entrusts to us.

Let's pray.

> Adonai, Lord and Master, thank you for your authority. I chose to submit and commit fully and completely to you. Thank you for the prayer of David in Psalm 125:1-2, "Those who trust in the Lord are like Mt Zion which

cannot be shaken but endures forever. As the mountains surround Jerusalem, so the Lord surrounds His people both now and forevermore." Thank you for the confidence and courage to do your will. In Jesus name, amen.

Day 8 Jehovah

When I think of a great work of art, I envision Michelangelo's magnificent rendering of God reaching out His finger toward the outstretched hand of Adam. The original fresco masterpiece adorns the ceiling of the Sistine Chapel in the Vatican, inside the boundaries of Rome, the capital of Italy. A copy of the same painting, hangs in my living room, a daily reminder of my personal God—Jehovah, God's most important name. This intimate name of God, Jehovah, represents the essence of God's being. Jehovah is unchanging, self-existent, and faithfully keeps His promises. Jesus said, "Before Abraham was I am" (John 8:58). Jehovah is our Redeemer, whose love for us never changes.

Is Jehovah the true name of God? The answer is found in the Hebrew Scriptures where the name of God is recorded as *YHWH*. So, where did the name "Jehovah" come from? When God revealed His name, I am who I am, he spoke his name using Hebrew verbs, not nouns. Ancient Hebrew did not use vowels in its written form. The vowels were pronounced in spoken Hebrew but were not recorded in written Hebrew. It is still not universally agreed upon how the Hebrew name for God *YHWH* was pronounced. Some prefer "Yahweh" (YAH-way); others prefer "Yehowah" or "Yahuweh"; still others argue for "Jehovah."

Regardless of the way Jehovah is pronounced, God answers to His name when we come before Him humbly as Moses did saying, "Yahweh here I am." These words of Moses show the face-to-face relationship he had with YHWH. Once God passed in front of Moses in a cloud proclaiming, "The Lord, the Lord, the compassionate and gracious God, slow to anger and abounding in lovingkindness and truth, who keeps lovingkindness for thousands, who forgives iniquity, transgression, and sin" (Exodus 34:6-7).

YHWH is God; there is none like Him. Encourage those around you to love Yahweh, live for Yahweh, and follow hard after him. Love the Lord your God with all your heart, mind, soul and strength. "Those who know Your name trust in You, for you, O Lord, do not abandon those who search for you" (Psalm 9:10 NLT).

Let's pray.

> Jehovah, Yahweh, thank You for revealing Yourself to me in a personal way. Thank You for taking initiative to reach out Your hand to me. I am thankful to know You and to be loved by You. Thank You for your presence, purpose, and peace in my life. Thank You that I can put my trust in You. I pray these words, "I have set the Lord always before me, because He is at my right hand I will not be moved" (Psalm 16:8). In Jesus name, amen.

Day 9 Jehovah Jireh

The cupboard was bare. We had nothing to eat except a small bag of long grain white rice and a couple of cans of refried beans. If we lived in Kenya, this would be a breakfast of champions, but at home in California, it seemed strange to serve it to my kids for their first meal of the day. Last night, we prayed about our empty pantry, I knew God would provide. And then, the doorbell rang. I opened the front door and said 'hello' to two bags of groceries. And yes, one bag contained a gallon of milk and a box of cheerios.

"So do not worry, saying, 'What shall we eat?' or 'What shall we drink?' or 'What shall we wear?' For the pagans run after all these things, and your heavenly Father knows that you need them" (Matthew 6:31-32).

Jehovah Jireh is the name of God that means The Lord Will Provide. God is willing and able to meet every need of His people. When we believe in God's provision, we are given hope blended with faith, and the result is trust. Abraham became acquainted with Jehovah Jireh in the greatest test of his life. The task was even bigger than when he left his home for an unknown land. God had fulfilled the promise of the birth of a son to aged Abraham and his barren wife, Sarah. And now, God asked Abraham to do the unthinkable—to sacrifice his precious and only son, Isaac, to God as an offering.

As Abraham raised his knife to slay his son, God provided the ram for the sacrifice in the place of Isaac, "Abraham named the place, "The Lord will provide" (Genesis 22:14).

We learned that Jehovah God offers His personal touch as He gives us intimate access to Himself. Here we see, "Jireh" as another adjective, God offering Himself as our provision by His specific method of deliverance.

God tested Abraham, which proved his faith as true, real, genuine, and authentic. When we pass this type of test, it always results in spiritual growth and blessing. God often works in the eleventh hour. God wants us to trust Him—to look for no solutions other than what He provides. When we know Jehovah Jireh, we trust Him to meet needs that can only be met by Him. Sometimes, it seems God takes His time answering, but God is never late, He is always working, and He will always come through for us. God will provide for every need we have, as we submit our needs to Him to meet them in His way, in His time.

Some of the greatest tests of our faith exhaust every possible resource, forcing us to look upon God's provision as our only hope. AW Tozer said, "The happy Christian has met the Lord personally and found Him an all-sufficient Savior and Lord. He has burned all the bridges in every direction."

Abram called the place Jehovah Jireh-The Lord Will Provide. "God will supply all your needs according to His riches in glory in Christ Jesus" (Philippians 4:19).

Let's pray.

> Heavenly Father, for each and every relationship, task or trial, You ask me to lay on the altar, I commit them to You. Jehovah Jireh, You are my personal deliverer. You are my provider, Almighty God. I have experienced Your provision over and over again. Thank You for the tests You have given

me. Thank You, Jehovah Jireh, for offering so many opportunities to trust You. I pray for Your strength as I wait and witness Your continued provision as You supply every need I have. I surrender, submit and sacrifice all upon Your altar. It's all for Your glory. In Jesus name, amen.

Day 10 Jehovah M'Kaddesh

I was glad when I was asked to play on the girls' softball team. It felt good to be wanted, needed and included. I remembered last season, I'd been overlooked, I waited to be picked and at the end of the selection process, I was not chosen until the end. I was the very last person to be invited to be on the team. It was horrible to feel left out.

We are specifically chosen by Him. We are set apart to be used by God. "Be holy, for I am holy," says the Lord. God would not give us this command if He didn't give us the power to do what He asks. Jehovah M'Kaddesh is the name of God that means "The Lord Who Sanctifies." The term was used first in Exodus 31:13 when God instructed Moses to teach the Israelites to observe the Sabbath. God is holy and by His Spirit's transforming power, we are set apart for Him.

Sanctification follows redemption. Sanctification is not only a singular work accomplished by Christ on the cross, but also an ongoing process within us, accomplished by Christ through the power of the Holy Spirit.

This sanctification; or separateness of life, is accomplished by the power of the Holy Spirit and the release of the living, active Word of God. Jesus final prayer for His disciples is found in John 17:17-19, "Sanctify them by the truth; your word is truth. As you sent me into the world, I have sent them into the world. For them I sanctify myself, that they too may be truly sanctified." AW Tozer said, "Holy is the way God is. To be holy He does not conform to a standard. He is that standard. Because He is holy, His attributes are holy, that is whatever we think of as belonging to God must be thought of as holy."

"I will give you a new heart with new and right desires, and I will put a new spirit in you. I will take out your stony heart of sin and give you a new, obedient heart" (Ezekiel 36:26). We are to live a holy life and shine as a light in this world. We belong to God. We are forgiven, set free, and set apart for the Lord—that we might live for His glory, holy and separate.

In *The Pursuit of Holiness,* Jerry Bridges said, "Our reaction to circumstances is part of our walk of holiness. Holiness is *not* a series of do's and don'ts. Holiness *is* conformity to the character of God and obedience to the will of God. Set apart and chosen, we are free to be the best possible version of ourselves."

Let's pray.

> Dear Jehovah M'Kaddesh, thank You for setting me apart for You. Thank You for fulfilling Your promise of sanctifying me and allowing me to live a holy life to shine Your light to the world. In Jesus name, amen.

Day 11 Jehovah Nissi

We ran for cover. The sudden tropical downpour lasted only five minutes, but we were as wet as if we'd been suddenly doused by heavenly buckets, soaked all the way through our clothes with puddles inside our shoes. We found welcome shelter under the canopy of the meeting tent.

In the same way, if we run for cover into the presence or under the canopy of Jehovah Nissi, we find shelter and protection from the storms, battles, and trials we face. Trusting in Jehovah Nissi gives us confidence in every struggle. In the heat of the battle, we need confidence and courage to prevail. Jehovah Nissi is the name of God that means "I Am the Lord Your Banner." Moses celebrated the Israelite's victory over the enemy by building an altar. "So Joshua overcame the Amalekite army with the sword" (Exodus 17:13). God revealed himself with a new name, "Moses built an altar there and named it The Lord My Banner" (Exodus 17:15). Jehovah Nissi wants us to praise Him for the victory He gives us in our trials. God gives victory against the flesh, the world, and the devil. Our battles are His battles of light against darkness and good against evil. Psalm 60:12 reminds us, "With God's help we will do mighty things, for He will trample down our foes."

The name of God, Jehovah Nissi is only used once in the Bible, but God's strong hand is seen throughout Scripture. He is a God of deliverance, the battle is His, the Lord will fight for us. David cried out to God in His distress and we can, too. In desperation, call out to Jehovah Nissi for help.

"The Lord also thundered in the heavens and the Most High uttered His voice…. He sent out his arrows and scattered them…. and he took me, drew me out of many waters. He rescued me from my strong enemy, and from those who hated me, for they were too mighty for me. They confronted me in the day of my calamity, but the Lord was my support. He brought me out into a broad place, he rescued me, because he delighted in me" (Psalm 18:13, 14, 16-19 ESV).

No matter what depressing thought, discouraging word, or diminished hope comes our way, let's choose to run for cover—to the Lord our Banner—Jehovah Nissi. He will shelter us, protect us and deliver us.

Let's pray.

Dear Jehovah Nissi, thank You for delighting in me. I thank You for anticipating my need to run for shelter. I love it when You cover me, defend me, and restore me to looking forward to the victory You will bring. Father, thank You for helping me trample my enemy. I give You the glory for the victory You will win. In Jesus name, amen.

Day 12 Jehovah Rohi

My friend Susan recently sent me a message, "Sheryl, I remember the day I heard the news your precious husband, Pastor Paul had been killed in the motorcycle accident. I rushed to your office to find out what happened. I couldn't believe it; Paul had died. And now, the same thing has happened to me. My beloved husband, Frank tragically died of a massive heart attack. It's so horrible. I can't believe it. Please pray for me."

My tears flowed for my friend's loss, understanding the shock of Susan's disbelief. I prayed, "Lord provide for Susan." Immediately, I sensed the tender care of Jehovah Rohi. He says, "I Am the Lord Your Shepherd."

Isaiah 40:11 explains, "He tends his flock like a shepherd: He gathers the lambs in his arms and carries them close to his heart; he gently leads those that have young." Jehovah Rohi leads us, guides us, and protects us as a shepherd leads His sheep. We must willingly let Him keep us close to His heart and trust Him to carry us.

In whatever circumstances, Jehovah Rohi lovingly watches over us as a shepherd guards his sheep. David, appointed to be the shepherd of God's people, knew he also needed his trustworthy shepherd in Jehovah Rohi. "The Lord is my shepherd, I shall not be in want. He makes me lie down in green pastures, he leads me beside quiet waters, he restores my soul." (Psalm 23:1-2). How can we handle the days, even years, we feel overwhelmed with loss, stress, or worries? We can be comforted with the fact that we have a Shepherd who cares for us. Jehovah Rohi will give us strength and peace to face the uncertain future that lies ahead.

Jehovah Rohi is possibly the most personal and precious name of God. The Hebrew words translated "The Lord is my shepherd" are Jehovah (Yahweh roi) first used by David in Psalm 23:1. After David's use of the title of shepherd, God is seen as the shepherd of his people in Isaiah as it refers to the greatness of God. In the New Testament, Jesus refers to himself as the Good Shepherd in John 10:11, the Shepherd and Guardian of your souls (1 Peter 1:25) and the Chief Shepherd (1 Peter 5:4), and the lamb who will be their shepherd (Revelation 7:7).

In the name Jehovah Rohi, we see an intimate relationship between the Shepherd and His sheep. The Shepherd protects, provides, directs, leads, and cares for His people. God tenderly takes care of us as a strong and patient Shepherd. "I am the good Shepherd, and I know my own and my own know me" (John 10:14 ESV). This status brings privilege and promise, "My sheep hear My voice, and I know them, and they follow me, and I give them eternal life, and they shall never perish. And no one can snatch them out of My hand" (John 10:27-28 ESV).

Would you join me as I pray for my friend Susan? But wait; while we are at it, there are so many others who have suffered tragic loss through a sudden death. So let's also pray for them, too. It is a comfort to know those who knew Jesus Christ as their personal savior are with Him in heaven, yet we also must remember that a sudden loss such as Susan's is a breeding ground for bitterness, depression, and even separation from our faith. It's difficult to find peace in the loss of dreams, departure from those we love, and disappointment in the sudden change of future plans, marriage status, financial status, and much more. We can serve our Lord—Jehovah Rohi, our Shepherd—by faithfully praying for the survivors of death. Here's a partial list of those who feel the pain: the grieving, surviving spouse, sons, daughters, siblings, parents, co-workers, neighbors, church members, and any others affected by the loss of their precious loved one.

Let's pray.

Dear Jesus, Thank You tender Shepherd, for Your sweet care for our loved ones, especially those who are suffering because of the death of their special loved one. Lord, I think of Susan, Kimberly, Shirley, and scores of others who are grieving. O dear Shepherd, provide for every need, may they not lack in any way. Lord, help them lie down and rest in luscious green pastures, lead and nourish beside quiet waters, restore and replenish souls.

Guide and direct them in paths of uprightness for your name's sake. Escort them as they walk through the valley of the shadow of death, keep them near in their faith, and draw them close to Your heart. Help them not to fear because You are with them. Not only will You defend them with Your rod and Your staff, this protection provides peace and comfort.

O Shepherd, thank you for your provision for physical needs as You feed them. Gracious shepherd, prepare a table of delicious food in the presence of enemies. Thank You for choosing to honor them as You anoint their heads with oil, keep their cups full to overflowing. Allow goodness and love to follow each day, so they may serve and love You in your presence. In Jesus precious name, amen.

Day 13 Jehovah Sabaoth

F acing any giants? These monstrosities could be looming over us, as we face times of difficulty, doubt, despair or depression. Or maybe disappointment, disease, destruction, divorce, discouragement, domestic violence or even death. Are you immobilized by a situation that seems too big? When David faced the Philistine giant Goliath, he said, "You come to me with a sword and a spear and a javelin, but I come to you in the name of the Lord of hosts, the God of the armies of Israel, whom you have defied" (1 Samuel 17:45 ESV). David's defender was 'the name of the Lord of hosts, the God of the armies of Israel." Talk about name-dropping! Remember the commercial "When E.F. Hutton talks, people listen?" When David spoke the name of the Lord of hosts, Jehovah Sabaoth, it got everyone's attention.

David faced an extreme encounter of the giant kind, and the Presence, Jehovah Sabaoth, the Lord of hosts, opened the way before him. Jehovah Sabaoth, the Lord of Hosts rules as the chief commanding officer of the armies of heaven. In the same way, Jehovah Sabaoth's authority and supremacy are more than enough for each of us, Jehovah Sabaoth avails His limitless power and boundless resources to us whenever we call on His name.

Old Testament believers found Jehovah Sabaoth's clout reliable; he delivered them when they asked. "He who forms the mountains—who turns dawn to darkness, and treads on the heights of the earth the Lord God Almighty is His name" (Amos 4:13). Today, Jesus emboldens us to take courage in the midst of tribulation, for He has overcome the world. Jesus is the overcomer and will give us strength in our difficulties. "But in all these things we overwhelmingly conquer through Him who loved us" (Romans 8:37NASB). This is Jehovah Sabaoth who delivers us from failure and defeat. "Not by might nor by power but by my spirit says the Lord of Hosts" (Zechariah 4:6 NASB).

Facing a giant today? Do a little name dropping. Let Jehovah Sabaoth, the Lord of Hosts, the commander of the armies of heaven defend you and your family. He will help you defeat your enemy.

Let's pray.

> Jehovah Sabaoth, you alone are in charge of everything, and the armies of heaven are at your command. Send me help. You are able to deliver me. Nothing I face today is greater than you. I can say these words with confidence because you are Jehovah Sabaoth. "I can do all things through Christ who strengthens me" (Philippians 4:13 NKJV). O Jehovah Sabaoth, you give marching orders to the armies of heaven, once again, I chose to surrender my life to Your command. Thank You that I can be strong in the Lord and in the strength of Your might. (See Ephesians 6:10.) In Jesus name, amen.

Day 14 Jehovah Rapha

You have cancer," announced Dr. Du. Immediately, my senses went numb, and the room began to spin. As the harsh reality set in, my mind reeled, *Cancer, me? How could that be, there's no cancer in my family.* I looked across the doctor's office at my husband, Paul. I said, "This is really bad." I remembered Romans 8:28, "And we know that in all things God works for the good of those who love him, who have been called according to his purpose." And then I made a choice—to give God more attention than the cancer.

Jehovah Rapha is the name of God that means, "I Am the Lord Who Heals." Trusting in Jehovah Rapha brings healing to our lives whether we are suffering physical or emotional ailments. Jehovah Rapha forgives and heals all of our sins. "He heals the broken-hearted and binds up their wounds" (Psalm 147:3 NASB).

God revealed Himself as Jehovah Rapha to Moses during a time of bitterness. The people of Israel had traveled from the Red Sea three days into the wilderness of Shur. There was no water. The people complained. Moses prayed, and the Lord made the bitter waters of Mara sweet. The people drank the water, and their thirst was quenched. Afterward, the Lord said, "I the Lord, am your healer" (Exodus 15:26 NASB). When we face the bitter trials of life, we have a choice: to complain or to praise God. The only one who can help us in the most intense times of trial and testing is the Lord Who Heals.

The Hebrew phrase, translated, "the Lord Who heals" is Jehovah Rapha and reveals God's ability to restore, to heal, and to cure. This healing not only comes in the physical sense but also in the moral and spiritual sense. The Hebrew root verb raphe (to heal) occurs approximately 70 times in the Old Testament.

To trust God for healing means to rely totally on Him. *Trust* means **T**otal **R**eliance **U**nder **S**tress and **T**rial. Can God heal? Yes. Will He heal? Yes. He is the Lord, the Great Physician. When we encounter disappointments, difficulties, or devastating disease, we can view them as opportunities to see how He heals. In June of 2004, I was given a diagnosis of stage 4 non-Hodgkin's lymphoma. This blood cancer showed up in five places in my body. The lymph node of my lower left eye-lid and the bone marrow of my right arm, shoulder, elbow and the femur of my left leg. We prayed to God for my healing, if it was God's will.

During my season of cancer, I studied the healing of the ten lepers in Luke 17. There were ten lepers who asked for healing. All ten were healed, but only one went back and thanked Jesus for that healing. After six months of chemotherapy, two surgeries, side effects, and lots of prayer, my oncologist, Dr. Risbud called, "Sheryl, I can't believe it, there's no more cancer!" Praise to Jehovah Rapha—my Healer. I was delivered from stage-4 cancer!

I want to be like that one leper who went back to Jesus to thank him. I borrowed this prayer of Moses from Psalm 90:12, "Teach me to number my days, that I might present to you a heart of wisdom." I thank God for delivering me from cancer. For giving my life back to me. Actually, it is His life to use for whatever purpose He wills it.

Through his son, Jesus, God has provided the final cure for spiritual, physical, and emotional sickness. Jehovah

Rapha makes us well. "O Lord my God, I cried out to You for help, and You restored my health" (Psalm 30:2 NLT). Cry out to Jehovah Rapha to forgive and heal all of your sins.

God gave His son, Jesus, to us as the most wonderful gift of courageous healing love we could receive. The encouraging words of John 3:16 tell us, "For God so loved the world, that He gave His only begotten son, Jesus, that whoever believes in Him should not perish, but have eternal life." God gave His son, Jesus, to the world as the only way we can have fellowship with God. Through relationship with Jesus Christ, we are healed and whole emotionally, physically, and spiritually. If you don't know Jehovah Rapha, he's waiting to meet you. Won't you pray this prayer today?

Let's pray.

> Dear Lord Jesus, you are Jehovah Rapha, the God who heals. I need Your healing in my life. I am sick and tired of being sick and tired. I know that I am a sinner and need Your forgiveness. I believe that You died for my sins. I want to turn from my sins. I now invite You to come into my heart and life. I want to trust and follow You as Lord and Savior. In Jesus name, amen.

Day 15 Jehovah Shalom

Lying awake at 3 am, thoughts rolled around in my mind along with conversations that should have happened. I felt a huge loss. My stomach was in knots—my heart twisting and turning about a decision that had been made for me. I had no say in the matter. I felt so alone in the inky blackness of the night, but then I called out to God, *Lord, I don't understand this at all, but I trust you, I submit to you, and ask you for peace.* Soon, I fell into a deep sleep. Waking up a few hours later, I knew Jehovah Shalom, the God of peace had taken over my mind. Instead of thinking in broken sentences, I now sang aloud with outrageous joy. The battle was won, I was confident, purposeful. He had chosen me for a greater work.

Jehovah Shalom is the name of God that means I am the Lord your Peace.

God called Gideon a mighty warrior during the time the Midianites attacked the Israelites. It was there God revealed Himself to Gideon in a new way, in revealing the name, Jehovah Shalom. Through the peace he received, he was able to find strength to lead his armies to victory. "Gideon built an altar to the Lord there and called it "The Lord is Peace" (Judges 6:24).

The Hebrew phrase translated "The Lord is Peace" is translated Jehovah Shalom and occurs only once in the Old Testament. Shalom is a "harmony of relationship or a reconciliation passed upon the completion of a transaction, the payment of a debt, giving satisfaction." The Lord is a God of peace even in the midst of overwhelming odds. Jehovah Shalom offers peace in every situation.

When you feel as if God has abandoned you, it helps to remember that He will be our peace. The only catch is that He wants us to ask for it. "Peace I leave with you; my peace I give to you; not as the world gives do I give to you. Do not let your heart be troubled, nor let it be fearful" (John 14:27 NASB). "You will keep in perfect peace those whose minds are steadfast because they trust in you" (Isaiah 26:3). "For He Himself is our peace…" (Ephesians 2:14).

"Gideon built an altar to the Lord there and named it, The Lord is Peace" (Judges 6:24). Jehovah Shalom gives peace in every situation but especially in those times when we feel lost, overlooked, weak, and inadequate. He keeps us in perfect peace when our minds are fixed on Him. (See Isaiah 26:3.) And that's the tough part; we must choose what we think about. Joyce Meyer says, "Say no to stinkin' thinkin'." Allow the peace of God rule in your heart, mind, and soul.

Let's pray.

> Heavenly Father, thank You that Jesus is my peace. When I have anxiety and fear I can pray Philippians 4:6-7, "Don't worry about anything, instead, pray about everything. Tell God what you need and thank Him for all He has done. If you do this, you will experience God's peace." Thank you for reconciling me to You, Lord, for peace of mind, divine favor. Thank You that like Gideon you say to me, "The Lord is with you, Mighty Warrior." In Jesus name, amen.

Day 16 Jehovah Tsidkenu

Self-righteousness can be viewed as a negative character quality. Remember "The Church Lady?" She was made famous on Saturday Night Live by actor Dana Carvey dressed as a religiously pious, yet prudish and frumpy elderly woman. So what was the point? The woman was squeaky clean in her behaviors, yet her attitudes were unlovely and a far cry from ethical. The Church Lady's attempt to be good actually worked against her, paving the way for her ego driven self-righteous piety to thrive.

Consider the word righteous. Even the most honest, ethical, moral individual could not be good enough to work their way into heaven. Jehovah Tsidkenu is our righteousness. "God made Him who had no sin to be sin for us, so that in him we might become the righteousness of God" (2 Corinthians 5:21). Because of the finished work of Christ, God sees us as righteous as He sees His Son. "There is no one righteous, not even one" (Romans 3:10). The meaning of 'tsidek' is straight, stiff, balanced, as on scales and full width, justice, right righteous, declared innocent. God is our righteousness. And this righteousness has been gifted to us through God's son, Jesus. "But now apart from the law the righteousness of God has been made known, to which the Law and Prophets testify. This righteousness from God comes through faith in Jesus Christ to all who believe" (Romans 3:21-22).

Google defines righteousness as "the quality of being morally right or justifiable." What a comfort to know that God provided for our righteousness. He knew we couldn't do it on our own. "For all have sinned and fall short of the glory of God, and are justified freely by his grace through redemption that came by Christ Jesus. God presented him as a sacrifice of atonement, through the shedding of his blood— to be received by faith." (Romans 3:23-25a).

When we accept Jesus as our Savior, His blood covers our sins, and He clothes us in His robe of righteousness. This outfit is perfect for any and every occasion. Aren't you glad we don't have to settle for the frumpy rags The Church Lady wears? Jehovah Tsidkenu—I Am the Lord Your Righteousness represents us before the throne of grace.

I am looking forward to the future. I can't wait for the day prophesied in Jeremiah 23:5-6, "'The time is coming,' says the Lord, 'when I will place a righteous Branch on King David's throne. He will be a King who rules with wisdom. He will do what is just and right throughout the land. And this is His name: The Lord Is Our Righteousness.'"

Let's pray.

> Dear Jehovah Tsidkenu, thank You for the blood of Jesus, the only Righteous One. He willingly died in my place, let His blood cover my sins, so I could be righteous, justified, restored to fellowship with You, my Holy One. Thank You for Your love, peace, purpose, and righteousness. I can't wait for the day when You rule the New Earth and finally make all things right. In Jesus name, amen.

Day 17 God of Heaven

I think about heaven a lot. Heaven is an eternal city called the "new Jerusalem." Imagine a crystal clear river flowing down the middle of the city, from the throne of God. On each side of the river, there will be a tree of life. The streets will be of purest gold, like translucent glass. Adorning the walls of the city will be every kind of jewel: emerald, onyx, amethyst, topaz. The Lord's presence will give the heavenly city the light it needs. "Give thanks to the God of heaven, his love endures forever" (Psalm 136:26).

It is essential to know who the God of Heaven is since everything on earth depends on it. There is only one God, although God is known by many different names. Each of His names displays aspects of His character and offer contact points to us through His personality.

Before rebuilding the wall at Jerusalem, Nehemiah petitioned God about his request, "Then I said: Lord, the God of heaven, the great and awesome God, who keeps his covenant of love with those who love him and keep his commandments" (Nehemiah 1:5).

Another worshipping pray-er, young Daniel, "… praised the God of heaven and said: 'Praise be to the name of God for ever and ever; wisdom and power are His'" (Daniel 2:19b-20).

The God of Heaven is also the God who rules over us. He is the One who has everything under control, even the circumstances we don't understand or don't like. It helps to give us perspective as we look forward to the future. Spending eternity in heaven is just a breath away.

The true beauty of heaven is explained:

"I saw the Holy City, the new Jerusalem, coming down out of heaven from God, prepared as a bride beautifully dressed for her husband. And I heard a loud voice from the throne saying, "Now the dwelling of God is with men, and he will live with them. They will be his people and God himself will be with them and be their God. He will wipe every tear from their eyes. There will be no more death or mourning or crying or pain, for the old order of things has passed away. He who was seated on the throne said, "I am making everything new!" Revelation 21:2-5

Let's pray.

> Dear God of Heaven, it's amazing that You would care about my problems. Thank you for helping me renew my perspective about spending eternity in heaven with you. Thank You for restoring my hope and renewing my trust in You. In Jesus name, amen.

Day 18 Zur

I live in California. Earthquakes are common talk. We wonder when "the big one" will hit. Earthquake preparedness is a must: schools participate in earthquake drills, companies host earthquake preparedness seminars, and individuals prepare earthquake survival kits. We try to be as prepared as we can for the inevitable. But when a 3.5 quake rattled our peaceful community, I was caught off guard. It happened early in the morning. I was in my bedroom making my bed, and suddenly the floor underneath my feet shifted down, like an elevator's sudden descent. I felt the downward motion and toppled sideways as my stomach did a flip. Around me, vases and books tumbled off shelves; pictures loosed from hooks, jumped off the wall. In an attempt to find stability, I slid down the side of my bed skirt, my rear end willingly hitting the floor. Now seated with legs crossed, with both hands I grabbed the nap of the shag carpet and held on for my life until the shaking stopped.

Maybe you've never been in an earthquake, yet we've all been in uncomfortable and unstable places more often than we'd like. I call these *life-quakes*. When we feel unsure in relationships, job, or finances, we face *life-quakes* that rattle our trust in God's stability. We wonder why, if God really loves us, He let the shaking start and why He doesn't make it stop. Circumstances make us feel like our comfortable little world is rocked, turned topsy-turvy, even dismantled. It is essential for us if we want to function in God's victory to remember Who is our foundation.

The name of God, Zur, means God our Rock. God wants us to hold onto His promises and stand firm in the power of His stable presence. We begin with the renewing our mind, which comes by reading His word, marinating in His promises, and standing on the solid ground God provides when we own up to our authority in Christ and rise up in faith.

Wikipedia defines rock as the solid mineral material forming part of the surface of the earth and other similar planets, exposed on the surface or underlying the soil or oceans. But the term rock is also used in similes and metaphors to refer to someone or something that is extremely strong, reliable, or hard.

Life-quakes hit when we least expect them. Since these times of being all shook up are part of life, and we know these inevitable quakes are coming, let's make a choice now to practice a little *life-quake* preparedness. Let's prepare for the big one and the small ones, too. When the *life-quake* hits, we will be able to find stable ground again. An added blessing is while we let God help us assimilate ourselves, we can also help others in the midst of their personal *life-quakes*.

First, we must implement the reaction of praising God and thanking God before He sends the solution and the shaking stops. God's nature is a firm foundation, so we can expect His consistent response as Zur – God Our Rock. When we trust Him, we anticipate His best is on the way to help us find our firm footing once again. Isaiah understood the concept of praising and thanking the Rock of Israel. "And you will sing as on the night you celebrate a holy festival; your hearts will rejoice as when people playing pipes go up to the mountain of the Lord, to the Rock of Israel" (Isaiah 30:29).

Some of us might be skeptical about the time it might take, because we want the shaking to stop, now. If you have a hard time believing your firm footing will be restored and that the shaking will stop, consider David's words, "The Lord is my rock, my fortress and my deliverer; my God is my rock, in whom I take refuge, my shield and the horn of my salvation, my stronghold" (Psalm 18:2).

Here's one more promise to claim, especially if you feel like you are on shifting sand. "He lifted me out of the slimy pit, out of the mud and mire; he set my feet on a rock and gave me a firm place to stand" (Psalm 40:2). Speak this verse several times as you wait for the shaking to cease!

Let's pray.

Heavenly Father, thank You for being Zur—God Our Rock. You love me. Thank You for helping me anticipate *life-quakes*. Let me prepare for the inevitable, as I understand Your character to help me stand firm. Thank You for your extreme strength, stable presence, and firm foundation. Help me to stay near to You, my Rock, my fortress, and my stronghold. In Jesus name, amen.

Day 19 Deliverer

Love covers a multitude of sins." The words rang in my ears, and I couldn't get the six-word phrase off my mind. At seventeen, already an alcoholic and an addict, I was working at a summer camp in Lake Tahoe. Although I was raised in church, I had never been around Christians like these. They didn't tell me to change anything about my appearance, my attitudes, or my addictions. "Love covers a multitude of sins," they said, when I smoked cigarettes or dope or threw fits over doing my chores. "Love covers a multitude of sins." Was God's love enough to cover *all* the wrong, illegal, and immoral things I had ever done, including my alcohol addiction, lying, bad habits, promiscuity, and even my drug dealing? Was it true that I didn't have to clean up my act before coming to God and that he loved me passionately just the way I was?

One night, in the quietness of my cabin, I submitted to the overwhelming love of God. I agreed with him about my condition and allowed his grace to cover my multitude of sins. That was June 1974, and God hasn't let go of me since. God delivered me from my drug and alcohol addiction.

"How quickly we forget God's great deliverance in our lives. How easily we take for granted the miracles he performed in our past." David Wilkerson

The name of God: Deliverer reminds us God will rescue us if we call on Him. He will give us victory over the most difficult circumstances and will see us through. "He rescued me from my powerful enemy, from my foes, who were too strong for me." 2 Samuel 22:18

When you need deliverance read Psalm 107, a beautiful song written about liberation. It was sung to celebrate the Jews' return from the freedom from bondage in Egypt and return from their exile in Babylon.

Remember Joseph's story? Through his brothers' jealous mistreatment, God allowed Joseph to be taken away as a slave to Egypt. He ultimately became Pharaoh's right-hand man and planned ahead for years of famine. He led the country to become the world's economic leader. Through Joseph, God provided for the Israelites to thrive in the land of Egypt. Decades later, there was a Pharaoh ruling who didn't know Joseph; God allowed the Israelites to be oppressed by the Egyptians. The Israelites grew in numbers and power, and the pharaohs began to eliminate them. Moses was sent by God to lead the Israelites to freedom.

"Give thanks to the Lord, for he is good; his love endures forever. Let the redeemed of the Lord tell their story…" (Psalm 107:1-2).

Thankfulness to God should always be on the lips of those whom he has saved. This verse is a beautiful picture of the response of the Israelites after they had been freed, though they deserved only judgment. They had been in bondage, yet the Lord heard their cries, and he freed them. A definition of redeemed found at answers.com says "redeemed means to extricate from an undesirable state: reclaim, recover, rescue." God rescued His people. The Israelites experienced the God who redeems.

Another definition is to "restore the honor, worth, or reputation of." *You botched the last job but can redeem yourself on this one.* What about you? Have you truly experienced what redemption means? We can trust God to redeem us in impossible circumstances and claim his promises.

"Then they cried out to the Lord in their trouble, and he delivered them from their distress" (Psalm 107:6).

God the Deliverer heard the cries of the children of Israel; He knew their situation. "The Israelites groaned in their slavery and cried out, and their cry for help because of their slavery went up to God. God heard their groaning and he remembered his covenant...so God looked on the Israelites and was concerned about them" (Exodus 2:23).

God promised deliverance in Exodus 6:6, "I am the Lord and I will bring you out from under the yoke of the Egyptians. I will free you from being slaves to them." God also said in verse 7, "I will take you as my own people and I will be your God. Then you will know that I am the Lord your God, who brought you out from under the yoke of the Egyptians."

God's people had cried out to God. They were in anguish because of their oppression. He heard them. God delivered them; he brought them out of slavery. He freed them from captivity. Have you cried out to God in your trouble?

When I was given a diagnosis of stage 4 non-Hodgkins lymphoma, I prayed to God for my healing and so did others around the world. We prayed, nights and days, we anguished in prayer for my healing. I was delivered from disease. I thank God for delivering me from cancer.

God wants to deliver you.

Are you worried about the future? Isaiah 40:31 is for you "Those who hope in the Lord will renew their strength."

Are you worried about the unknown test results, finances, a prodigal child? Isaiah 54:10 is for you "though the mountains be shaken and the hills be removed, yet my unfailing love for you will not be shaken, nor my covenant of peace be removed."

And when the Deliverer carries you through, thank Him and praise Him for the satisfaction He brings. "Let them give thanks to the Lord for his unfailing love...for he satisfies the thirsty and fills the hungry with good things" (Psalm 107:8-9).

Hope in things = Distracted

Hope in people = Disappointed

Hope in myself = Devastated

Hope in Christ = Delivered

Rachel Wojo

Let's pray.

> Heavenly Father, we give thanks to You, for You are good. "Your love endures forever. Let the redeemed of the Lord tell their story" (Psalm 107:1-2). Thank You for hearing my cries, as I cry out in time of trouble. Thank You for delivering me. (Psalm 107:6) Thank you Lord, for your unfailing love. Thank you for satisfying the thirsty and filling the hungry with good things. (Psalm 107:8-9) Thank you My Deliverer, You are so good. Thank You, My God. In Jesus name, amen.

Day 20 El Kanna

Ever had a jealous boyfriend or jealous mother? Sometimes possessive jealousy can bring on fierce damage especially in relationships gone bad. But that is not God's kind of jealous.

The name of God, El Kanna – Jealous, might seem negative since usually, we think of jealousy as bad. Jealousy can mean green with envy or lust—we don't have something someone else has so we covet it.

The first commandment reads: "I am the Lord your God, who brought you out of Egypt, out of the land of slavery. You shall have no other gods before me" (Exodus 20:1-2). The commandment was given to the children of Israel for their good, to give them guidelines for living. God understood their desire for worship. Held in captivity in Egypt, they'd become familiar and even intrigued with other gods. Some Israelites worshiped foreign man-made pagan gods, providing opportunity for the Living God to give instructions for right living via The Ten Commandments in Exodus 5:6-21.

At first, the Israelites followed the Ten Command-ments and obediently worshiped God whole-heartedly. With enthusiasm, they built the tabernacle, ordained priests, of-fered sacrifices, and burned incense, yet their love for God drained and their focus waned. Moses was summoned to Mt. Sinai, to meet with God, to receive the Ten Commandments written by God on stone tablets. Now the people impatiently waited for Moses to come down the mountain, complained and groaned about their lot, took matters into their own hands. Exodus 32:1 shows us what they said, "Come, make us gods who will go before us." Aaron gave orders to begin making a golden calf for the people to worship. The Lord warned Moses what he was going to find when he returned from Mt. Sinai. Yet Moses sought God's favor and pleaded with Him to have mercy, "O Lord, why should your anger burn against your people, whom you brought out of Egypt with great power and a mighty hand?" (Exodus 34:11). God heard Moses pleas and sent His mercy. God didn't change His mind, but God changed His behavior in a way that was consistent with His nature. Because of His love, God's mercy was unleashed.

Because of mercy, God's anger was withheld, yet Moses wrath was released as he smashed the tablets. Then, he burned the golden calf, ground it into powder, scattered it onto water and made the Israelites drink it. A second time, the Lord asked Moses to join him at Mt. Sinai to receive two new stone tablets. It was there Moses petitioned the Lord, "O Lord, if I have found favor in your eyes, then let the Lord go with us. Although this is a stiff-necked people, forgive our wickedness and our sin and take us as your inheritance" (Exodus 34:8-9).

The Lord knew then, as He knows today, that other gods will compete for our hearts. He is fully aware of the wiles of the enemy who wants to exploit that unquenchable longing for more. "Then the Lord said, I am making a covenant with you. Before all you people I will do wonders never before done in any nation in all the world" (Exodus 34:10). "Do not worship any other god, for the Lord, whose name is Jealous, is a jealous God" (Exodus 34:14).

The word jealous makes us think of words like envy, resentment, or rivalry. But it also means vigilantly guarding something, intolerant of unfaithfulness, or righteous zeal. The name El Kanna expresses God's desire to be first in our hearts and lives. He desires for us to vigilantly guard our relationship with Him and to remain faithful to Him as He zealously pursues us. El Kanna alone is worthy of all our devotion and praise. He wants to be number one. He is jealous for us because He made us, loves us, and wants us for His own.

I had the privilege to attend Beth Moore's worldwide "Audacious" simulcast along with 150,000 other women. Beth taught about "Six Mighty Makers," to help us grow closer to God. Mighty Maker number one is, "The audacity to make an unseen Savior the supreme romance of your life." That's what loving a jealous God is all about, because God's jealousy is more about us than about Him. You and I are on His mind all the time. He made you for the express purpose of sweet fellowship with Him. God doesn't want to share you with any other god. He is not willing to make a threesome of it. Do you know any wife willing to share her husband with another woman? Are you aware of a husband who would be okay with his wife running off on a Hawaiian vacation with another guy? Yep, that's our God. He is jealous for us. He wants us all to Himself. And I like it that way.

"Place me like a seal over your heart, like a seal on your arm; for love is as strong as death, its jealousy unyielding as the grave" (Song of Songs 8:6).

Let's pray.

Heavenly Father, thank You for Your grace, mercy, and compassion for us. We love You El Kanna—our Jealous God, thank You for being mindful of us. Help us keep You on our minds all the time. "Love the Lord your God with all your heart and with all your soul and with all your strength" (Deuteronomy 6:5). Thank You for drawing us to You, even when we become distracted by other things or people and we give them more of our attention than we give You. Thank You for your love and strength. In Jesus name, amen.

Day 21 El Bethel

I couldn't wait to get to my secret place. I had found it the first day I'd arrived at the Christian camp. I'd stumbled upon it when I was searching for a camper who'd gotten separated from our group. I remembered how the ancient oak tree's sanctuary beckoned me into its peaceful canopy; its trunk twisted into a natural seat provided me solace during my camp counselor summer job watching over hundreds of noisy children. The oak tree was my hallowed spot, my sacred area and sanctuary.

One of my favorite things about studying the names of God is how God reveals Himself to us through the characteristics associated with His name. For the name, "El Bethel," I think of how real God was to Jacob, just at the time Jacob needed it. God became Jacob's sanctuary, his secret place, his hallowed spot. Jacob was running away from his brother, yet our more-than-enough God reiterated the promise for Jacob's future and also provided a way of escape. In the same way, God proves Himself to us over and over if we give Him a chance. Whenever we need Him, all we have to do is ask for His help. "Call to me and I will answer you and tell you great and unsearchable things you do not know" (Jeremiah 33:3).

The name El Bethel occurs only once in the Bible. It's the name that Jacob gave to the place near Bethel where he had seen the famous ladder from earth to heaven. The word *El* is either a semi-personal name of God or the commonly accepted abbreviation of Elohim. God of Bethel, the name of the place where Jacob had the vision of the ladder, and where he erected an altar.

Jacob had a dream. In it, he saw a stairway to heaven and the angels of God were climbing up and down the steps. The Lord stood at the top of the stairway and spoke to Jacob, "I am the Lord, the God of your father Abraham and the God of Isaac. I will give you and your descendants the land on which you are lying. Your descendants will be like the dust of the earth, and you will spread out to the west and to the east, to the north and to the south. All peoples on earth will be blessed through you and your offspring. I am with you and will watch over you wherever you go, and I will bring you back to this land. I will not leave you until I have done what I promised you" (Genesis 28:13-15).

Can you imagine a dream such as that? What an amazing experience, to see the angels going up and down the ladder to heaven and then to hear God's voice audibly. No wonder, Jacob went back to the same place and built an altar to commemorate the event.

"So Jacob and all the people with him came to Luz (that is, Bethel), in the land of Canaan. There he built an altar and he called the place El Bethel because it was there God had revealed Himself to him when he was fleeing from his brother" (Genesis 35:6-7).

Maybe you haven't been visited by God in a dream, lately, but you've had a recent answer to prayer. Why not ask God to show you how to remember the answer? It helps to write down the time and place the answer came, and you can even take it a step further and set up an area of remembrance. In *The War Room* movie, Miss Clara has a "Wall of Remembrances." There she posted the answers to prayer. What a wonderful way to give God the glory and also remind ourselves of how God has worked in our lives. God knows how short our memories are. We need reminding to remember God always answers prayer.

Let's pray.

> El Bethel abide in me. Set up Your home in the very depths of my soul. Let Your words dwell in me that I may know and live by them and for You. Reveal to me the sin I must confess and turn from that I may be pure and blameless in Your sight. Show me how to best honor You through this temple which You have set up within me. Guide me in my eating habits, in my entertainment choices, and even in what I wear so that in your house – El Bethel – which is in me may glorify you in all that I do. Grant me the discernment to know how to reflect you.[4]

Day 22 God of Israel

Do you wonder if God can handle your problems? A proper perspective of God's magnificence helps us trust that He is much better at managing things in our lives than we are. But wait, there's more. God wants all men and women, boys and girls, from every tongue, tribe, and nation to know His love. "O Lord, God of Israel, there is no God like you in heaven or on earth —you who keep your covenant of love with your servants who continue whole heartedly in your way" (2 Chronicles 6:14). Appearing 195 times in the Old Testament, this name of God shows the Lord's sovereign rule over the nation and people of Israel.

According to google.com, "God of Israel may refer to God in Judaism, God as understood in present-day Jewish theological discussion." And yes, the people of Israel are God's chosen people. But God loves and has a plan for all people. God loves people. He wants everyone to have the opportunity to know Jesus Christ as his or her personal savior.

Isaiah, the prophet, had a vision of the Lord of hosts on His throne; "In the year of King Uzziah's death I saw the Lord sitting on a throne, lofty and exalted, with the train of His robe filling the temple. Seraphim stood above Him, each having six wings: with two he covered his face, and with two he covered his feet, and with two he flew. And one called out to another and said, 'Holy, Holy, Holy, is the Lord of hosts, The whole earth is full of His glory'" (Isaiah 6:1-3 NASB).

The prophet wrote, "O Lord of hosts, the God of Israel, who is enthroned above the cherubim, You are the God, You alone, of all the kingdoms of the earth. You have made heaven and earth" (Isaiah 37:16 NASB). Now that's proper perspective. Did you know approximately 16,300 ethnic people groups are considered unreached, less than 2% Christ-followers, that's over 41% of the world's population?[5] The body of Christ is the vehicle God is using to share His love with the nations. This fulfills His purpose in availing His plans, power, and presence with all who will receive Him. "The Lord is not slow in keeping His promise, as some understand slowness, but is patient toward you, not wishing for any to perish, but for all to come to repentance" 2 Peter 3:9).

"How beautiful on the mountains are the feet of those who bring good news, who proclaim peace, who bring good tidings, who proclaim salvation who say to Zion Your God reigns" (Isaiah 52:7).

Yes, the God of Israel is able to handle our problems. Yes, the God of Israel wants to use us as part of His plan to invite all men and women into His family of love. When Isaiah received his call as a prophet from the Lord of hosts, Isaiah responded, "Here am I. Send me!" (Isaiah 6:8). Will you answer God's call in the same way?

Let's pray.

> Heavenly Father, God of Israel, thank You, there is no God like You in heaven above or on earth below. You are our creator, our promise-keeper, worthy of our worship and praise. You are not willing for any man or woman, boy or girl, no matter their tongue, tribe or nation to die without the opportunity to join Your family of love. Today, God of Israel, we commit to use the time, talents, and treasure You have entrusted to us for your

glory. Show us how to share the truth that all men and women, boys and girls may hear, see, and understand Your great and mighty love. In Jesus name, amen.

Day 23 Ancient of Days

Ilove hymns. I remember belting out this chorus as a youngster, "Our shield and defender, the ancient of days, pavilioned in splendor and girded with praise.[6]

So what does this name of God, Ancient of Days mean? "The title 'Ancient of Days' first appears in Daniel 7:9, where Daniel is describing his vision of heaven. There an ancient, or venerable, Person sits on a flaming throne with wheels of fire, His hair and clothing white as snow. The flaming throne is symbolic of judgment, while the white hair and title 'Ancient' indicate that God existed before time began. In Isaiah 43:13, we find that God refers to Himself existing from ancient of days (literally, before days were). That means God existed before days were even created. We read in Genesis 1 that God created time, days and nights, so God existed from before the beginning of time. God is often represented as ancient, as He that is "from everlasting to everlasting" (Psalm 90:2) and as 'the first and the last' in Isaiah 44:6."[7]

The title Ancient of Days is found only three times in Scripture, all three in prophetic passages in Daniel 7:9, 13, and 22. Verse 22 refers specifically to Jesus whose judgment will be part of the end-times events. In Daniel 7:13, the term "ancient of days" refers to God the Father, and we see Him on His throne as Jesus, the Son of Man approaches the throne on clouds. God is a triune God, meaning three persons in one, and at different times Ancient of Days refers to Jesus Christ, and at other times the name applies to God the Father.

In the prophetic sense, it clearly refers to Jesus, the Ancient of Days, returning to pronounce judgment on the world. (See Daniel 7:22.)

So what does the term "ancient of days' mean to us today? Authority, supreme authority, belongs only to God the Father both in heaven and earth. God the Father will judge all mankind through His son, Jesus Christ. We will each have to appear before the Judgment Seat of Christ (See Romans 14:10; 2 Corinthians 5:10.), and the judgment we receive will determine our eternal destiny.

The Ancient of Days loves you and has a plan for your life. God's love is unconditional; God's love is perfect. How do we know God loves us? "But God demonstrates His own love for us in this, while we were still sinners, Christ died for us" (Romans 5:8).

God created us in His image—for a relationship with Him—but He gave us freedom of choice, to partake in the love relationship with Him or not. The problem is, we are separated from a Holy God because of our sin. "For all have sinned and fall short of the glory of God" (Romans 3:23). "For the wages [payment)] of sin is death, but the gift of God is eternal life in Christ Jesus our Lord" (Romans 6:23).

There is only one solution for the problem of separation from God…some have tried to earn their way to heaven by working harder or being religious, but "Without the shedding of blood, there is no remission [forgiveness] sins" (Hebrews 9:6).

Jesus Christ is the only answer to the problem. He died on the cross and rose from the grave, paying the penalty for our sin. He provided a way for us to have a relationship with God.

As you read John 3:16, pause at the blanks to say your name aloud and fill in the blank. "For God so loved _____ that He gave His only begotten son, that if _____ believes in Him, _____ should not perish, but have everlasting life" (John 3:16). What amazing love.

God sent His son, His only son Jesus, to die for us. Which one of us would give our children—our only child— for the lives of someone? God did, for you. Imagine God making a way for you to be restored into a relationship with Him by giving His only Son as a sacrifice.

You must make the choice. Are you separated from God? I want you to be totally honest before God. Is there any reason why you cannot receive Jesus right now?

God has loved you since before the beginning of time. He gave you a gift. His son Jesus Christ died for you on the Cross and rose from the grave. Jesus cares for you, and He calls you, to make a decision for Him, today. He has a plan for your life. Don't miss out on the life God has for you.

We can't clean up our act ourselves. I know. I've tried. God has allowed Jesus blood to cover our sins, so we can have fellowship with Him.

"If we confess our sins, He is faithful and just and will forgive us our sins and purify us from all unrighteousness" (1 John 1:9).

God is asking you to give yourself totally and completely to Him. Pray this prayer to invite Jesus Christ to come in and control your life through the Holy Spirit.

If you have already received Christ at one time in your life but feel you would like to recommit your life and your family to Christ, you can pray this prayer, too.

Would you pray this prayer with me?

Dear Lord Jesus,

I know that I am a sinner and need your forgiveness.

I believe that You died for my sins.

I want to turn from my sins.

I now invite You to come into my heart and life.

I want to trust and follow You as Lord and Savior.

In Jesus name, amen.

I am so glad you decided to receive Jesus as your savior. It is the best decision you've ever made. I look forward to spending eternity with you and the Ancient of Days.

Day 24 Jehovah Jashopet

I feel so dirty," my friend sobbed. "I feel like everyone is criticizing me." It was the end of our weekly recovery support group meeting and for the previous hour, the dear lady had vulnerably shared her painful past. Our group of four had compassionately listened, loved, and prayed over her past mistakes. "How can God forgive me for aborting my child?" Like so many others, this sweet woman was trapped in her guilt, shame, and blame. She was her worst judge.

Jehovah Jashopet is the name of God that means The Judge. The adjective righteous describes His most important attribute as a judge. In the Bible, the words for righteousness and justice are closely related. The name Righteous Judge includes the idea that God judges justly. The Message Bible calls Him the honest Judge, and elsewhere He is also the God of justice. God's justice will never be swayed by bribes or altered by irrational grudges. God's righteousness includes punishment of the guilty, but it leaves room for His mercy and forgiveness toward repentant sinners.

In the book of Judges, the *shophetim* (judges) were clearly rulers and deliverers, not just those who make legal decisions as they are today. (See Judges 11:27.) When the Bible uses the name, Righteous Judge, it includes all those meanings. Other names for God mention the different roles of God's involvement in the justice system: The Lawgiver and judge, or simply our Lawgiver. He also punishes the wicked.

Jesus (*Yeshua*) put judgment in perspective. Jesus did not come to earth to judge people; He came to bring salvation. However, there will be a final judgment by the Righteous Judge, and He will base that judgment on how we responded to Jesus' words.

"If anyone hears my words but does not keep them, I do not judge that person. For I did not come to judge the world, but to save the world. There is a judge for the one who rejects me and does not accept my words; the very words I have spoken will condemn them at the last day" (John 12:47-48).

The dear lady in my support group had loved God from an early age. She had accepted God's forgiveness of her sins, but she couldn't forgive herself. For decades, she was a willing participant in an ugly and painful game she could not win. She played the shame-game, placing herself in God's position, her mind repeating thoughts like, "How could I have allowed the unhealthy behavior to continue?" Like a merry-go-round she couldn't get off of, she worried circles around the blame-game, "Everything was my fault, I signed off on the abortion. I killed my baby." The judgmental thoughts she condemned herself with were like poison darts and affected her self-perception. You might struggle with the same lie, or perhaps the lies you believe differ.

Holding close to truth is the way we root out deception and take God at His word. We must devote ourselves to search out and find truth. This means we are dedicated to learn what God thinks about us. We must let God judge us, give him permission to convict and with His help, allow room to make changes. When we refuse to judge ourselves, the impact of our opinions and accusations of others will be diminished. God helped my friend untangle the knots of self-deception so she would be free to experience His truth. God's Word cut through the lies and ushered in the truth of

His love: "I have loved you with an everlasting love. I have drawn you with loving-kindness"(Jeremiah 31:3). When she heard, applied and believed what God said about her, she could love herself and accept even her past mistakes. When you feel guilty, it is difficult to move forward. But we don't have to be victimized by our past, held captive to our thoughts or imprisoned by how others perceive us.

Trusting God moves us ahead unhindered; our progress becomes secure as we apply God's word to our circumstances and allow Him to move us from deception to truth. It helps to take control of our thoughts and say His word out loud. The truth of Romans 8:1 break through guilt, shame, blame, and unworthiness, "Therefore, there is now no condemnation for those who are in Christ Jesus." Let God defend you and free you through the power of His word.

Let's pray.

> Dear Heavenly Father, thank You for sending Your son, Jesus (*Yeshua*) to put judgment in perspective. Thank You Jesus did not come to earth to judge people. But to bring salvation so everyone will live with him in heaven, forever. In Jesus name, amen.

Day 25 Jehovah Hamelech

As a youngster, I remember watching the movie *The King and I,* envisioning myself as the special woman who stole the king's heart. At the time it seemed appealing to be 'found' and then to become royalty. I am a hopeless romantic. A marriage to a king seems romantic because it would mean instant royal status.

King is a title given to royalty. Some of the kings I've heard of are biblical: King David, King Solomon, and King Jehosaphat. Current day kings I'm aware of are Burger King, the band - For King and Country, Martin Luther King and Elvis Presley. Jehovah Hamelech is the name of God which means The King. Our God is King, Our God reigns! Let's honor him as Lord and King, the high and lofty one. He is absolute, sovereign over his people, Ruler of All Things, Prince, Potentate, Majesty on High. When God revealed himself to the patriarchs, it was as God Almighty or God Most High. To Moses it was Yahweh, I am. When the Israelite nation was brought out of Egypt, God revealed himself as their King. The Song of Moses concludes with the triumphant 'ruling' words:

"The Lord will reign for ever and ever" (Exodus 15:18).

This is the first time in the Old Testament that *mālak* occurs with God as its reference. It means, "to reign, to be and exercise functions of a monarch, whether male (king) or female (queen)."

Melek is by far the most common word in the Old Testament for chief magistrate or ruler and is usually translated "king, lord, captain, ruler, prince, chief. The *title* of King for God doesn't appear much in the Pentateuch, but the *symbolism* of Exodus makes it clear that Israel was to see Yahweh as their King.

Jesus promised us, his followers, that we would inherit the kingdom of God. Can you imagine the impact this truth would have on us if we lived in the reality of the words in this verse? "The Lord will be king over the whole earth. On that day there will be one Lord and his name the only name" (Zechariah 14:9). Very soon, we will live in a marvelous place where there will be worship, love, peace. We will be loved, accepted, understood, and included. I don't know about you, but this gives me renewed resolve and re-aligned perspective on how I will serve Jehovah Hamelech – the King.

Here are a few more future promises from our King about His coming Kingdom where you and I will live with Him for eternity.

"The righteous will shine like the sun in the kingdom of their Father" (Matthew 13:43).

"Then the King will say to those on his right, 'come you who are blessed by my Father, take your inheritance, the kingdom prepared for you since the creation of the world" (Matthew 25:34).

"Then I saw a new heaven and a new earth, for the first heaven and the first earth had passed away, and there was no longer any sea. I saw the Holy City, the new Jerusalem, coming down out of heaven from God, prepared as a bride beautifully dressed for her husband. And I heard a loud voice from the throne saying, 'Look! God's dwelling place is now among the people and he will dwell with them. They will be his people and God himself will be with them and be their God. He will wipe every tear from their eyes. There will be no more death or mourning or crying or pain, for the old order of things has passed away'" (Revelation 21:1-4).

Now it is 'the King and I,' but not on the movie screen. It is me and Jehovah Hamelech. A future kingdom awaits us. I am more than excited and highly motivated to make a difference today as I serve my King and build His kingdom together with you until His return.

Psalm 98:6 says "with trumpets and the blast of the ram's horn, shout for joy before the Lord, the king."

Let's praise our King.

> Dear Lord, you are King of kings and Lord of lords. Thank you for your strength and presence as almighty ruler, our great King. In Jesus name, amen.

Day 26 El Birith

Ever been disappointed in a loyal friend? Frustrated with lack of follow through on a commitment? Or worse yet, has someone close to you broken a promise?

Of course, all of us have experienced these kinds of pain. Unfortunately, people we trust go back on their word regularly, severed contracts and fragmented vows are an everyday occurrence. El Birith is the name of God that means God of the Covenant. Used of Baal in Judges 9:46. Probably used originally to refer to the God of Israel – Baal-Berith.

The idol Baal-berith was worshiped by the Jews after the death of Gideon. It was identical with Baal-zebub, "the ba'al of flies," the god of Ekron. This idol was shaped like a fly. The Jews were so addicted to this cult that they would carry an image of the idol in their pockets, producing it and kissing it from time to time. Ba'al-zebub is called Ba'al-berith because the Jews were known to make a vow of devotion to the idol and refused to be apart from it for a single minute.

Sounds disgusting. To carry around an image of a fly in your pocket for the purpose of caressing, worshiping, and even kissing. As a person who has recovered from a list of chemical dependencies, I am prone to becoming addicted to other things I might think could help me manage my stress. There is something I carry in my purse that is a temptation and sits on the fence of becoming an addiction. I may not 'kiss' my iPhone, but I pay too much attention to it when I am constantly checking it. I've decided to put boundaries on eyeing my iPhone.

I will pray that we allow ourselves to be consumed with claiming God's promises so that we are not dependent on anything or anyone for handouts to make us feel better about ourselves. The only One who keeps every promise He has ever made to us is our covenant God El Birith.

Our God is a covenant God. He always keeps His promises. Even when the fulfillment of these promises is still in the future and unseen, Christ-centered hope must be the foundation of our lives. Hard times come and hard times go, but God's promises are forever. Here are a few verses for you to keep with you,

"When I am afraid, I will trust in you. In God, whose word I praise, in God I trust; I will not be afraid. What can mere mortals do to me?" (Psalm 56:3).

"Trust in Him at all times, you people; pour out your hearts to him, for God is our refuge" (Psalm 62:8).

"Yet this I call to mind and therefore I have hope: because of the Lord's great love we are not consumed, for his compassions never fail. They are new every morning; great is your faithfulness. I say to myself, 'The Lord is my portion, therefore I will wait for Him'" (Lamentations 3:21-24).

"How joyful are those who fear the Lord and delight in obeying His commands. Their children will be successful everywhere; an entire generation of Godly people will be blessed" (Psalm 112:1-2 NLT).

Let's pray.

Dear El Birith, You are the God of the Covenant. Thank You for keeping every promise You have ever made to me. Help me to meditate on Your word today, claim Your precious promises, so I may focus on You and Your will. Thank You for Your faithfulness. In Jesus name, amen.

Day 27 Jehovah Shammah

A loud crash woke me up from a deep sleep. I opened my eyes, squinting to sort through the all-encompassing shadows as if blinking my eyes would dissipate the thick, inky, suffocating blackness. There was no difference from when my eyes were closed. I couldn't see anything. I didn't remember where I was. I cried out to God, *Help me, Lord.* Immediately I felt peace, comfort, and hope in the shelter of God's presence. Instead of feeling breathless from fear, a sigh of relief became my prayer of thanksgiving and praise. "Thank you Jehovah Shammah."

This peace gave me fortitude to get up and investigate the source of the loud crash. I was relieved to find one of my hanging pictures had pulled off its grip from the wall hanger and lay in pieces on the floor. No intruder had crashed in one of my windows. Whew.

Jehovah Shammah is the name of God that promises His presence. Corinthians reminds us, "you are a temple of God and the spirit of God dwells in you." Deuteronomy 31:6 says, "the Lord your God is the one who goes with you, He will not fail or forsake you."

Imagine this scene: The Temple had been built as a place for God to dwell. The Israelites were deep into worshipping other gods, but God had given them numerous opportunities to repent from their rebellion. They stubbornly refused. God withdrew His presence not only from the temple but also from the city of Jerusalem. He was so angry over their repeated rebellion that He said, in effect, "I've had it. I'm out of here."

God promised the nation would be restored, and His presence would return to Jerusalem. The city would be called Jehovah Shammah. Prophesy was fulfilled when God's presence returned to the temple. The way it happened wasn't at all what anyone expected. God's presence was restored to Jerusalem in the form of a tiny baby brought to the temple to be offered back to God by his parents, Joseph and Mary.

Jehovah Shammah is found Ezekiel 48:35, "The distance around the entire city will be six miles. And from that day the name of the city will be 'The Lord is There.'" Jehovah Shammah is the name of God that means I am the Lord who is there and is symbolic of Jerusalem. This name promises His presence. God wants us to experience His presence every moment of every day.

Jehovah Shammah is the God who is there. Our God is already in our tomorrows. "'For I know the plans I have for you,' says the Lord. 'They are plans for good and not for disaster, to give you a future and a hope'" (Jeremiah 29:11-12 NLT).

"Do not fear, for I am with you; do not be dismayed, for I am your God. I will strengthen you and help you; I will uphold you with My righteous right hand" (Isaiah 41:10).

God is here for us, now. The Holy Spirit is our reminder that God is here for us, He is closer than a brother. "I am with you always, even to the end of the age" (Matthew 28:20).

Jehovah Shammah is the God who is here for all of us who cry out, today, tomorrow, and forever.

Let's pray.

Dear Jehovah Shammah, thank You for being the One who goes with me. Thank You for the hope I have that You will not fail or forsake me. Thank You for the strength I find in Your presence today. In Jesus name, amen.

Day 28 Father of the Heavenly Lights

Ever taken astronomy? I remember when I found out there are names for the thousands of constellations, I was amazed to find there were even more galaxies and solar systems beyond ours. Even the sun, moon and stars had a beginning. They are the heavenly lights; God created each and every one of them. An overlooked name of God is Father of the Heavenly Lights. Sun, moon, and stars are the common terms for the illuminators of our atmosphere. Imagine the scene when they were created: "And God said, 'Let there be lights in the vault of the sky to separate the day from the night, and let them serve as signs to mark sacred times, and days and years, and let them be lights in the vault of the sky to give light on the earth. And it was so" (Genesis 1:14-15).

Despite the fact that God spoke these luminosities into being, I marvel in amazement at the sheer concept of light. The word is defined as a noun in dictionary.com: "Light is something that makes things visible or brings clarification: All colors depend on light. Light is defined in physics as luminous energy and radiant energy. Light is the thing that causes our eyes to react. Light is an illuminating agent or source, as the sun, a lamp, or a beacon."

God had great plans for the sun and the moon. In fact, he designed specific job assignments for each one. "God made two great lights—the greater light to govern the day and the lesser light to govern the night. He also made the stars. God set them in the vault of the sky to give light on the earth, to govern the day and the night, and to separate light from darkness. And God saw that it was good" (Genesis 1:16-19).

Every spectacular sunrise is an offering of God's affection, a daily reminder that God is still on His throne. Each moonlit night draped in a velvety sky dotted with twinkling stars is created for our delight and God's glory. It's no wonder God expresses His desire to give us more favors, "Every good and perfect gift is from above, coming down from the Father of the heavenly lights" (James 1:17). God gives good gifts to His children. He created the stars and moon to light the night. In the same way, He will shine His hope by offering His presence anytime we need it, but especially on our darkest days of depression and hopelessness. Thank the Father of Heavenly Lights.

Our Heavenly Father is the most generous person in the universe; He gave His only son for us. Let every breath we take remind us our life is a gift from Him. Now that you know more about this name of God, "Father of Heavenly Lights," how will you invite your Father of Heavenly Lights into the dark places of your life? If you ask, the One who gave birth to the sun, moon, and stars will begin to push away your dark clouds of despair. How will you respond to the giver of everything you have and are?

Let's pray.

> Father of Lights, thank You for Your plan and promise for my life. Thank You for every good and perfect gift You have given me. Thank You for the opportunity to share how generous You are. I give You all the glory and praise. In Jesus name, amen.

Day 29 The Sun of Righteousness

Imagine a burning globe fueled only by the righteousness of God. It can't shine any brighter or burn any hotter. The sun of righteousness is a name for God that appears in Malachi 4:2 "But for you who revere my name, the sun of righteousness will rise with healing in its wings. And you will go out and leap like calves released from the stall." This blessing is promised to those who fear the Lord and are ready for His return.

"Sun of righteousness" can also be translated "son of vindication." The context concerns the Day of the Lord, the time when God vindicates His people and judges sin.

The One described as the "sun of righteousness" can be no other than Jesus Christ Himself. The Lord is called "the Lord your righteousness" in Jeremiah 33:16. And the coming of the Messiah is pictured as a sunrise in several passages. "Arise, shine, for your light has come, and the glory of the LORD has risen upon you" (Isaiah 60:1 ESV).

The fact that the sun of righteousness rises with healing in its wings invokes the picture of the wings of a bird stretched across the sky, offering healing to those below. A healing effect will infuse the earth during this time, removing the negative impact of past sins. (See Isaiah 30:26; 53:5.) When Christ returns, God's righteousness and peace will flood the earth.

God's desire has always been to provide righteousness to those who trust Him. God's people were said to be "clothed in righteousness." In Malachi 4:2, God's people will see the Sun of Righteousness Himself rising over the world. It's a picture of the future millennial reign of Jesus Christ. The darkness of the Antichrist's reign will vanish, and the light of God will take its place. It's a new day dawning; God's people will revel in their freedom.

Let's pray.

Dear Heavenly Father, your holiness and righteousness amaze me. Thank you, Sun of Righteousness for blessing me with your nearness as you burn up all the hurt and hate with your presence. Thank you for your purpose and peace. I look forward to your reign as you bring wholeness and hope to all who trust you now. In Jesus' name, amen.

Day 30 Jehovah Maozi

I was a little late. Heads turned as I walked into the crowded Sunday school classroom. I'd had my last chemotherapy session just two days before, and everyone knew it. The group around the coffee and donuts dissipated as people moved my way. "Honey, how are you doing?" Lucy gingerly inquired. And then cautiously Betty wondered, "How are you feeling?" And finally, Sharon reprimanded, "I thought you should stay home and stay in bed today."

These were concerned friends, almost like family, yet I felt like an innocent child getting a bad scolding. As a stage-four cancer patient, I was fighting for my life. I wanted everything to be back to normal and I was tired of being a cancer patient—and the attention it brought me. I felt out of control. I understood these greetings, and bits of advice were meant to encourage, but instead they cut deep like sharp daggers.

My friends' intent was to show their concern, but it was too much attention for me. And then others decided I needed to hear their advice and opinions about cancer's side-effects, diagnosis, and treatment. It didn't feel good when they told their own relative's death-by-cancer story or documented the most up-to-date information on the current cutting-edge treatment. I needed a sign that said, "I'm doing very well, under the circumstances. It's good to see you, too. I appreciate your continued prayers." I prayed God would help me be compassionate and gracious.

That day, I was surprised how the meant-to-be-encouraging words made me feel so wounded. I'm not sure why, other than how it seemed the comments were tossed out carelessly. Where could I run? I thought about making a quick trip to the women's room. Who could I turn to? It seemed no one safe was readily available. *God help*, I prayed. Then I remembered a song I taught my kids when they were in elementary school. "The name of the Lord is a strong tower; the righteous man runs into it and is safe." (See Proverbs 18:10.) And so that's what I did, I ran into the Lord's presence.

I asked God to shelter, protect me, and heal me from the hurtful comments and misplaced opinions of those who meant well. I turned to God to be my fortress.

Defined, a fortress is a strong tower that can't be moved. It's a stronghold. God is a protective haven of shelter from harm, but He can only be this for us if we choose to run to Him for safety, He is our safe place. He knew we would need a place to run. "The Lord is my rock, my fortress and my deliverer, my God is my rock, in whom I take refuge, my shield and the horn of my salvation, my stronghold" (Psalm 18:1-2). I chose Jehovah Maozi to be my fortress, my protector. Instantly, I felt his peace and was delivered from the pain of the hurtful comments.

No matter what you are facing today, Jehovah Maozi—my fortress provides his presence. Let Him be a dwelling place you can go for help. His presence is a refuge; His peace has impenetrable walls. Wherever we are, we can run to our fortress' He is waiting for us to come to Him so He can comfort us. Nothing and no one can harm us when we abide with Him and He with us.

"He who dwells in the shelter of the Most High will abide in the shadow of the Almighty. I will say to the Lord,

'My refuge and my fortress, My God, in whom I trust.'"
(Psalm 91:1-2 ESV).

Let's pray.

> Dear Jehovah Maozi, You are my fortress.
> Thank You for protecting me from physical
> and emotional harm. Help me to run to You,
> at the exact time when I need Your presence to
> enfold me. Help me to seek You immediately.
> Thank You for Your name, that it is a strong
> tower. Help me to run to it and allow You to
> keep me safe. In Jesus name, amen.

Day 31 Alpha and Omega

"Everything but the kitchen sink" or "A to Z" means from beginning to end.' Alpha and Omega is a powerful name of God. "'I am the Alpha and the Omega,' says the Lord God, 'who is, and who was, and who is to come, the Almighty'" (Revelation 1:8). Jesus is here declaring himself to be everything from A to Z and in complete control of history. Alpha is the first letter of the Greek alphabet and Omega is the last letter. The Lord God is the beginning and the end. When he returns for his second coming, He will do so with all power and majesty in contrast to His first coming as a humble servant. All the Christian world awaits and joins the voice of the Apostle John, "Even so, come, Lord Jesus!" (Revelation 22:20).

Remember the name El Olam is the name of God that means He is eternal, without beginning or end, he is infinite. The infinity symbol, a mathematical symbol is sometimes used to illustrate the eternal concept of God. So how can God be eternal, yet at the same time have a definite beginning and end? Revelation 22:13 explains, "I am the Alpha and the Omega, the First and the Last, the Beginning and the End." God says he is the beginning of all things and the end of all things. God is the creator of time. He is beyond time itself, yet at the same time, He inhabits time. He is in control of the span of time, from His and time's beginning throughout eternity, infinity and beyond.

Are you totally confused? This concept might seem to twist your brain into a pretzel of contrasts, yet this reminds us that God is beyond our comprehension. (Job had a lengthy discussion with God about this.) God answered him, "Where were you when I laid the earth's foundation? Tell me if you understand. Who marked off its dimensions? Surely you know! Who stretched a measuring line across it?" (Job 38:4-5).

Is there any question in our minds that God can be trusted with the daily struggles of our lives from our first newborn cry to our last breath? Absolutely not.

"Behold, he is coming with the clouds and every eye will see Him, even those who pierced Him; and all the tribes of the earth will mourn over Him. So it will be. Amen" (Revelation 1:7 NASB).

Alpha and Omega. The First and the Last. The Beginning and the End. From A to Z. Our God is the beginning of all things and the end of all things. On that day when this old earth has ceased to exist, when there is a new heaven and a new earth, there will be a day of the New Jerusalem. Alpha and Omega will be seated on the throne and make everything new. Today, we can stand on the finished work of the cross of Christ. "He said to me, 'It is done, I am the Alpha and the Omega, the Beginning and the End. To the thirsty I will give water without cost from the spring of the water of life. Those who are victorious will inherit all this, and I will be their God and they will be my children'" (Revelation 21:6-7).

Let's pray.

> Alpha and Omega, thank You for who You are. I praise You for the mysteries of Your being. Thank You for the plans You have for mankind. I praise You for being the First and the Last. Thank You for including me in the

eternal purpose You have for the world. Help me to continue to be a light to the world so that all men and women may know Jesus Christ as Lord. Even so, come, Lord Jesus! Amen.

Bibliography

1. Arthur, Kay, <u>Lord, I Want to Know You,</u> 1992, 2000, Colorado Springs, CO, Published by Waterbrook Press, pp. 46, 81

2. Bright, Bill, <u>God: Discover His Character,</u> 1999, Orlando, FL, Published by New Life Publications, Pp. 41, 1272

3. Bright, Bill, <u>God: 13 Steps to Discovering His Attributes,</u> 1999, Wheaton, IL, Published by New Life Publications, Pp. 6 – 25

3. Bright, Bill, <u>God: Knowing Him By His Names,</u> 2000, Wheaton, IL, Published by New Life Publications, pp. 4 – 30

4. Martin, Catherine, <u>Trusting the Names of God,</u> 2008, Eugene, OR, Harvest House Publishers, Pp. 174, 181, 190

5. Purnell, Dick, <u>Knowing God By His Names,</u> 1993 Nashville, TN, Thomas Nelson, Inc. Publishers, Pp. 37, 60, 66, 72, 118, 119

6. Stone, Nathan. <u>Names of God,</u> 1944, Chicago, IL, Moody Bible Institute, Pp. 20, 122, 136

7. Sumrall, Lester. <u>The Names of God,</u> Kensington, PA, Whitaker House, Pp. 25, 51, 74, 121, 129

8. Spangler, Ann, <u>Praying the Names of God,</u> 2004, Grand Rapids, MI, Zondervan, Pp. 27, 99, 177, 251

9. Wong, Amy Ng, <u>Guide To God,</u> 2002, Uhrichsville, OH, Barbour Publishing, Pp. 96, 116

10. Ancient of Days, Robert Grant 1833, Public Domain, www.hymnary.org

11. www.MomsinPrayer.org/prayersheets

12. El Bethel Pinterest prayer www.pinterest.com/ pin/467248530068836332/

13. Answers.com   http:answers.com   Is Jehovah the true name of God? Jehovah – 8/21/2015

14. Google

    http:google.com – God of Israel – 10/5/2015

15. Wikipedia   http: www.wikipedia.com - Eternity – 8/12/2015, El Birith – 10/23/2015, King – 10/21/2015, Zur - Rock – 9/21/2015, Jehovah Shalom – 9/11/2015,

16. The Blue Letter Bible   http:www.theblueletterbible. com – El Shaddai – 8/17/2015, Adonai – 8/19/2015, Righteous – Tsidek – 9/14/2015,

17. http:www.simplybible.com – Judge – 10/19/2015

18. http:www.gotquestions.com – Ancient of Days – 10/9/2015

About the Author

Exchanging hurt for hope is Sheryl Giesbrecht's focus—a message she shares with audiences as a radio personality, author, and speaker. A dynamic teacher and motivating leader, Giesbrecht has endured many changes and challenges, moving her to a deep faith, trust, and dependence on God.

She served as Focus on the Family's columnist for Pastor's Wives for four years. Hundreds of her columns and magazine and devotional articles have appeared in Focus on The Family Magazine, Just Between Us, Discipleship Journal, CCM, Walk Thru the Bible's - InDeed and Tapestry publications. Sheryl contributes to Crosswalk.com and is a regular blogger for BibleGateway and Lead Like Jesus.

Giesbrecht's radio show, "Transformed Through Truth," can be heard each weekday evening on KAXL 88.3 FM Music for Life (www.KAXL.com) now nationally syndicated and heard daily by over 21 million listeners on networks across the United States (www.wilkinsradio.com).

She has a heart for missions and is avid about reaching out to the poor and needy, locally through the Rescue Mission and worldwide through Compassion International. Giesbrecht is a missionary with International Christian Ministries (www.icmusa.org). She has been personally involved with equipping hundreds and facilitating the training of thousands of leaders internationally. It is a ministry in which she worked alongside her late husband, Paul. Sheryl, who loves to encourage and coach leaders, is founder of Transformed Through Truth, Inc., a non-profit specializing in mentoring through transformation discipleship.

The joys of Giesbrecht's life are her adult children and their spouses, plus the new beginning she shares in her marriage to Dr. Jim Turner. Sheryl enjoys baking chocolate chip cookies, running in the foothills, and walking the dogs with her husband and their thirteen grandchildren. Sheryl holds a bachelor of arts from Biola University, a master's in ministry and a doctorate of theology.

www.From AshesToBeauty.com

www.TransformedThroughTruth.com

(Endnotes)

1   Nathan Stone, *Names of God*, Moody Publishers 2010, p 12

2   Lester Sumrall, *Names of God*, Whitaker House 2006, p 53

3   Bill Bright, *Knowing Him By His Names*, New Life Pubns 2002

4   El Bethel Pinterest prayer www.pinterest.com/pin/467248530068836332

5   (www.TheJoshuaProject.com)

6   Ancient of Days" by Robert Grant (1833), Public Doman, www.hymnary.org Access date: 1/15/2014

7   www.From Got Questions.org Access date: 10/09/2015